Cook It Light
PASTA, RICE, AND BEANS

Cook It Light
PASTA, RICE, AND BEANS

Jeanne Jones

Color Photography by Jim Coit

MACMILLAN • USA

MACMILLAN
A Simon & Schuster Macmillan Company
1633 Broadway
New York, NY 10019

MACMILLAN is a registered trademark of Macmillan, Inc.

Library of Congress Cataloging-in-Publication Data
Jones, Jeanne.
Cook it light pasta, rice, and beans / Jeanne Jones : color photography by Jim Coit
p.   cm.
Includes index.
ISBN: 0-02-862150-6
1. Cookery (Pasta)   2. Cookery (Rice)   3. Cookery (Beans)   4. Low-calorie diet—Recipes.
5. Low-fat diet—Recipes.   6. Salt-free diet—Recipes.
I. Title
TX809.M17J66   1994
641.8'22—dc20   93-1501
CIP

Paperback Edition 1998

Macmillan Publishing books may be purchased for business or sales promotional use.
For information please write: Special Markets Department, Macmillan Publishing USA,
1633 Broadway, New York, NY 10019.

10   9   8   7   6   5   4   3   2   1

Printed in the United States of America

This book is dedicated with thanks and deep appreciation
to the millions of people who read my column, "Cook It Light," each week.
Your letters are a constant source of challenge and
inspiration for everything I do.

CONTENTS

ACKNOWLEDGMENTS

Tracy DeMas, recipe testing; William Hansen, manuscript preparation and editorial assistance; Ginny Grandinetti, nutritional analysis; Viola Stroup, editorial research; Pam Hoenig, editor; Justin Schwartz, editorial assistance; Margaret McBride, literary agent.

INTRODUCTION

To reiterate what I've said in my dedication, this book would not be possible without the continuing input from the millions of people who read my column, "Cook It Light," each week. The letters I receive from readers requesting healthier versions of their favorite recipes are a constant source of challenge and inspiration.

This book, just like *Cook It Light* and *Cook It Light Classics,* is truly born of my column! It reflects the more healthful versions of the types of recipes my readers are most eager to have revised. Because I have recently received so many requests for revisions of pasta, rice, and bean recipes, I decided to devote an entire book to these popular complex carbohydrates.

As well as being among almost everyone's favorite foods, pasta, rice, and beans are extremely important nutritionally. They are a valuable source of fiber, contain no cholesterol, and are very low in fat.

When any legume (bean or pea) is combined with any grain (rice, pasta, etc.) it forms a complete protein. This combination is very important in a vegetarian diet. It is also important when trying to balance your meals to conform to the new food pyramid that lists complex carbohydrates as our most important food source.

Pasta, rice, and beans are also economical. There are no better meal extenders to mix with fish, poultry, or meat. In fact, I can't think of better examples of foods that can successfully stretch food dollars.

Rather than including an introduction to each chapter in this book, I am adding detailed information on pasta, rice, and beans as a part of this introduction. It seems more appropriate in that they are the main theme in every chapter, whether served alone or with fish, poultry, or meat.

PASTA

No one knows for sure exactly when or where pasta was invented, but China is its most likely birthplace. There is evidence that the Chinese were making wheat noodles as early as 100 B.C., and since then pasta has become the most popular staple in the world.

Perhaps the best reason for pasta's popularity is that it is so economical. After all, it was invented by people to whom richer foods, including fish, poultry, and meat, were either unavailable or often in very short supply. Therefore, sauces and seasonings were developed to add variety as well as flavor to the various types of pasta. Pasta is still one of the most inexpensive and nutritionally sound ways of extending the amount of animal protein served for a meal. Isn't it wonderful that preparing more healthful dishes can also save us money!

You can have lots of fun experimenting with the many different sizes and shapes of pasta available—or even try making your own. The more familiar Italian pasta shapes are usually divided into categories. Long round pastas include spaghetti and vermicelli, and also spaghettini and capellini, or angel hair, which are much smaller diameter pastas.

The long flat pastas include linguine, which is about one eighth inch wide, fettuccine, about one fourth inch wide, and pappardelle, which is about one inch wide. Also in this category is the lasagna noodle at about two inches in width. All of the long round and the long flat noodles, with the exception of lasagna, are usually served with a sauce. Lasagna is usually baked in a casserole with other ingredients such as tomato sauce, cheeses, and often meat in between each layer of pasta.

Tubular-shaped pastas, such as ziti, penne, rigatoni, and elbows are often used in soups as well as with sauces thin enough to fill the inside of the pasta. Larger-sized tubes such as cannelloni and manicotti are usually stuffed and baked.

Corkscrew or spiral-shaped pastas such as fusilli or rotini are wonderful for making pasta salads and casseroles because the ingredients cling to the extra surface area of the ridges on the pasta.

Other popular shapes include shells of various sizes, orecchiette (a round disk that is slightly hollow in the middle), farfalle or bow-ties, rotelle (little wheels with spokes), and orzo, which is shaped like rice. The smallest pastas, such as pastina and the Middle Eastern couscous, are as fine as cereal. They work well in soups and as side dishes.

Generally speaking, imported dry pastas are superior to American pastas because they are made from 100 percent semolina (the flour made from hard durum wheat). It doesn't absorb as much water as pastas made from all-purpose flour and, therefore, it has a firmer texture when cooked.

Fresh pasta has become increasingly popular in this country in the last few years. They can be found in specialty shops and many supermarkets. The advantages of fresh pasta include faster cooking time and a variety of flavors and colors. The disadvantages are that it is more expensive, usually contains eggs (and cholesterol), and must be used immediately. I use both dry and fresh pastas in recipes in this book because I think they both have merit, depending upon the recipe you are making.

Stuffed pastas such as tortellini and ravioli are best when you make them yourself, and must be made with fresh pasta. They are also available commercially, however. I must confess I almost always use the readily available oriental pasta, won ton wrappers, for making ravioli, which brings us to the oriental pastas.

Asian noodles of all types are now available in most supermarkets and add greatly to the wealth of pasta selections. While Western pastas are almost exclusively made with wheat flour, the noodles of the orient are extremely diverse. They use buckwheat, rice, mung beans, potato starch, and even sweet potatoes and yams to make their pastas.

Wheat noodles are usually associated with China and Japan, rice noodles with Southeast Asia, and dang myun, a gelatinous noodle made with the starch of sweet potatoes, with Korea. Also popular in Japan are soba, a hearty noodle made with buckwheat flour.

COOKING TIPS

Always cook pasta in plenty of rapidly boiling water. A teaspoon of salt may be added to the water, if you desire, but it is not necessary. You should use four to five quarts of boiling water for every pound of pasta being cooked. Stir the pasta as soon as it is dropped into the water, and keep stirring it to prevent the pasta from sticking together. Don't add oil to the pot because it will coat the pasta and cause it to repel, rather than absorb, your sauce.

The most important thing to remember is to never overcook pasta. It should be al dente, or resistant to the bite. Always follow the cooking instructions given on the package. Fresh pasta cooks in much less time than dried pasta, so watch it carefully.

Once cooked, quickly drain the pasta in a colander just until still slightly moist. Overdrained pasta rapidly becomes too dry. Also, never rinse pasta unless it is going to be used in a dish that will be further cooked in the oven, such as lasagna (see page 79).

Cooking times for oriental noodles vary greatly depending on the variety of noodle you're using. For example, rice noodles and bean threads should be soaked for about 20 minutes before cooking. Thin varieties need to be warmed, not boiled, or they will become a gelatinous mass. Thicker types need 1 to 5 minutes of boiling. When they turn transparent they are cooked. Again, always follow the package directions carefully—hopefully, they will be in English!

RICE

Although it is not known exactly where rice originated it is assumed that it was somewhere in Southeast Asia. The earliest records of rice as a crop date back almost 8,000 years in China. In fact, it was the Chinese who discovered that rice grows more abundantly underwater and started keeping their fields flooded during the growing season.

The growing of rice spread to Japan about 1000 B.C. and from there to the Middle East. Alexander the Great can be given credit for introducing rice to the Western world. He discovered it in India and brought it back to Greece in about 326 B.C. From there it made its way into Spain and Italy and eventually to their colonies in North and South America. However, rice production in the United States didn't begin until the last part of the sixteenth century.

Today rice is one of the world's most important foods. It accounts for up to 70 percent of the total calories consumed in parts of Asia and is applauded for its versatility the world over. Rice also gets high marks in nutrition. It contains no cholesterol, only a trace of fat, and provides about 160 calories per cooked cup. Also, fewer people are allergic to rice than to wheat or most other grains.

There was a time when the only choice we had readily available was either brown or white rice. Until the beginning of the nineteenth century, hand milling brown rice into white rice was such a labor-intensive process that white rice was associated with the wealthy and privileged, and brown rice was the rice of the masses.

After the Industrial Revolution, when white rice was cheap enough for virtually everyone, brown rice quickly became a rarity throughout the world. It has only been during the last twenty years that the "natural foods" and nutrition-conscious segment of our population has helped reestablish the importance of brown rice as a valuable food source. Now there are many varieties of rice from which to choose, which makes rice even more exciting from a culinary standpoint.

Brown rice has only the inedible outer hull or husk removed, leaving the bran layers intact. It is tan in color and has a nutty flavor and slightly chewy texture. It is also called "whole rice" because none of the nutrients have been removed. It provides significant amounts of fiber, vitamins, and minerals.

White rice was once brown. The difference is that the outer bran layers have been polished off. The outer layers contain so much of the fiber, vitamins, and minerals that the polishing by-product is sold for cattle feed and for the manufacture of vitamin concentrates.

Brown and white rice come in three sizes. Long-grain rice is three to five times as long as it is wide. When cooked, it tends to be lighter and fluffier than either medium-grain or short-grain rice. Medium-grain is two times as long as it is wide and cooks to a fairly fluffy consistency. However, as it starts to cool it begins to get sticky. Short-grain rice is less than two times as long as it is wide, making it almost round. It is higher in starch than long- or medium-grain rice and tends to be more moist. This makes it easier to eat with chopsticks and, for this reason it is the preferred rice in the Orient.

Converted rice (a trademark of Uncle Ben's) is parboiled rice which has been steamed under pressure. This returns some of the water-soluble nutrients from the bran that would normally be lost during processing back into the rice. This rice is firm and yields fluffy separate grains when cooked.

Aromatic rice is a term used for several varieties which have a strong, nutty aroma. Included in this category is basmati, grown primarily in India, Sri Lanka, and Pakistan, and jasmine rice, grown originally in Thailand but now also grown successfully in the United States. Also in this category are pecan rice grown in Louisiana, Texmati, a hybrid of basmati and long-grain rice, and Wehani, a brown rice with a rust-colored bran that splits when the rice is cooked and looks like cooked wild rice with a rust color.

Arborio is a wide-grain rice, slightly translucent with a "pearl" of opaque white at its core. It is perfect for making risotto. As it cooks, the translucent exterior dissolves, releasing its creamy starch to the developing sauce. The opaque core becomes tender and slightly chewy. In Venice, this texture is often described as chewy rice floating in a sea of cream.

Valencia rice is a medium-grain rice grown in the province of Valencia in Spain. It is a soft rice, similar to arborio, that soaks up flavor but remains firm in the center. It is a favorite in Spain for paella.

Sticky rice is sometimes called glutinous or sweet rice. The grains contain a high percentage of amylopectin, the starch that makes the grains stick together when cooked. It is most often used in Asian desserts. There is also a sticky black rice, available in Asian markets, which is a gorgeous deep purple color when cooked.

Wild rice is really not a rice but the seed of an aquatic grass. It was originally found growing in the shallow waters in the Great Lakes region by Native Americans in the first century A.D. They called it manomin, meaning "good berry." Today it is also cultivated in California. It is higher in protein than white rice and contains the amino acid lysine, which most other grains lack. The nutty flavor is developed by the processing technique. It is first fermented at a warm temperature then parched to caramelize and slightly brown the green seeds before being removed from the grass.

COOKING METHODS

Before cooking any rice always wash and drain it, removing any small rocks or bits of foreign matter from the rice paddy that may be left in it. The three most commonly used cooking methods for all types of rice are the covered pot, microwave, and rice cooker. In the covered pot method you bring the water to a boil, stir in the rice, and bring the water back to a boil. At this point you cover the pot and cook the rice over low heat, without lifting the lid, until the water is absorbed and the rice is the desired consistency.

Often the cooking instructions will also include a ten- to twenty-minute "resting" period after the rice is removed from the heat, and before the lid is lifted, to allow the rice to finish absorbing any moisture remaining in the pot. When the lid is finally removed from the pot, gently fluffing the rice with a fork will allow the steam to escape and keep the grains separate. Otherwise, rice should never be stirred while it is cooking (except for risotto) or it will become mushy. The cooking times and amount of liquid called for will vary with the kind of rice being cooked and the final texture desired. Always refer to the package instructions or the ingredients and method of the recipe being prepared.

You can reduce the cooking time of brown rice by about twenty minutes if you soak the rice in water overnight before you cook it.

Soak 1 cup of rice in 2 cups of water. The next day, drain the rice thoroughly and cook by the covered pot method in 2 ½ cups fresh water until the rice is tender, about 25 minutes.

Rice can also be prepared in your microwave. Since microwave ovens vary considerably in size and power, always refer to the manufacturer's guide when cooking in one.

Electric rice cookers are very common in most modern Asian kitchens and are increasing in popularity in the United States, as well. They are the most convenient and foolproof way of cooking rice. Rice cookers usually require slightly less water than conventional cooking methods. Follow the manufacturer's directions for use.

BEANS AND PEAS

Just as pasta is the broad category into which all rolled and extruded doughs are placed, regardless of shape or size, and rice is the category into which all of the approximately 40,000 varieties of this grain are placed, legumes is the category into which all beans and peas fall. Yet, until rather recently, you seldom heard the word "legumes" used at all.

Legume is a French word derived from the Latin, *Leguminosae* (meaning pod-bearing) for the family of plants that produces pods which split open as they mature, releasing their seeds. Legumes date back to prehistoric times when early man subsisted on whatever he could hunt or gather. They were also among the earliest plants to be cultivated.

There is evidence that the first domesticated crops were grown in Southeast Asia as early as 9750 B.C. By about 8000 B.C. chick-peas, lentils, and fava beans were being cultivated in the Middle East. Sometime around 6000 B.C. legumes were being grown in Mexico and by the Incas in Peru. Throughout the Middle Ages legumes staved off hunger when bad weather destroyed the grain crops.

Today legumes are still a major factor in feeding the world's population. They are also now getting their rightful recognition as one of the most healthful and nutritious foods available. They are high in complex carbohydrates, fiber, viatmins, and minerals. They are also low in fat and sodium, and contain no cholesterol, yet they are very high in protein. When combined with grains, seeds, nuts, or dairy products, they become a "complete" or usable protein essential in vegetarian diets and a healthy and innovative way to stretch food dollars for everyone.

Though the recent rise in popularity is certainly broadening our selection of beans and peas enormously, of the approximately 13,000 species of legumes, only a relatively small number of them are successfully grown and marketed. The most economical beans are the larger commercial crops bred for high yields and resistance to disease and fungus such as pinto, navy, kidney, Great Northern, lima, black beans, and black-eyed peas. However, many of the exotic "designer" beans are getting a great deal of attention in the culinary world as chefs compete with each other to be the first to discover either a new variety or an almost forgotten heirloom bean or pea.

The following is a description of some of the more commonly used beans as well as a few of the more readily available designer varieties:

Adzuki beans are small, oval, dark red beans with a white ridge. They have been grown and eaten in China and Japan for centuries and can be eaten fresh, dried, canned, sprouted, or ground into flour in savory dishes as well as desserts.

Appaloosa beans are a new pinto hybrid from the Palouse area of the Northwest. They are a large and creamy white bean with a black splotch and can be used in any recipe calling for pinto beans.

Black beans are medium-size oval beans also known as turtle beans. They are earthy and sweet with a hint of mushroom flavor and are a favorite in Latin American countries as well as on the menus of many upscale restaurants in this country.

Black-eyed peas, also called cowpeas, are a creamy white kidney-shaped bean with a dark purple, almost black, eye. They are popular in Southern, African, and Indian dishes and are available fresh, dried, frozen, and canned.

Cannellini beans are large, Italian white kidney beans with a nutty taste and smooth texture. They are often in used Italian dishes, especially salads and soups, and are available both in dry and canned forms.

Cranberry beans are round and plump beans that are used both fresh and dried. The pretty mottling of the dried bean disappears when cooked. They may also be called Roman beans and shellouts.

Fava beans are possibly the oldest variety of bean and are also called broad beans or horse beans. They are a very large bean, pale green when fresh and reddish-brown, dried. They have a nutty taste and granular texture and are used frequently in Italian, Middle Eastern, and Greek cooking. They have a very tough skin, which should be removed by blanching before cooking.

Garbanzo beans are another ancient bean also referred to as chickpeas. They are pale gold and round with a beaklike sprout, firm texture, and mild, nutlike flavor. They are most often used in African, Asian, Middle Eastern, and Italian cuisine—most commonly in salads, soups, and stews.

Great Northern is a large white bean that resembles the lima bean in shape, but it has a delicate and distinctive flavor. Great Northern beans are especially popular in baked bean dishes and can be substituted for any white bean in most recipes.

Kidney beans most commonly range in color from dark to light red, but can also be brown, white, or black. They also come in a variety of sizes and are favored for their robust flavor that holds up well in dishes like chili con carne. They are most often available dried or canned.

Lima beans also come in several sizes. The larger bean, or Fordhook, is more robust in flavor, and the dried variety may also be referred to as butter beans in the South. The smaller, buttery-textured baby limas are actually a separate botanical classification—they don't grow up to become Fordhook lima beans!

Mung beans are small, round ancient beans most often used for bean sprouts. They need no presoaking and can also be used dried, either whole or split. They have a tender texture and slightly sweet flavor when cooked. Dried mung beans are ground into flour to make noodles in China and a variety of dishes in India.

Navy beans are small, white oval beans also known as Yankee or pea beans. The bean gets its name from the fact that it has been a staple in the U.S. Navy for over a hundred years. Navy beans require lengthy, slow cooking and are widely used for commercially canned pork and beans. They are also wonderful in soups.

Peanuts are not a nut, they are a legume! Though we may think of them as rather common, the ancient Peruvians considered them a worthy food for their journey to the hereafter. The two most popular varieties of peanut are the Virginia and Spanish peanut. Refrigerate unshelled peanuts, tightly wrapped or in a sealed container, for up to six months. Peanuts are high in fat and rich in protein.

Peas occur in many varieties. The English pea, or common garden pea, is grown to be removed from the pod and eaten fresh. The field pea is grown specifically to be used dried, such as in split pea soup. The snow pea and sugar snap pea are meant to be eaten fresh, pod and all.

Pink beans are smooth, reddish brown beans, similar to both kidney and pinto beans. They are available in dried form year-round in most supermarkets and can be used in any dish calling for pinto beans.

Pinto, the Spanish word for "painted," is currently America's most popular bean. It is a squarish oval shape with streaks of reddish-brown on a background of pale pink, and available in dried form year-round. It is most often served with rice or used in soups and stews. Both the pinto and pink bean are commonly used in the preparation of refried beans and chili con carne.

Red beans are popular in Mexican and southwestern cuisine. They are a dark red, oval bean similar to a kidney bean. They are available, dried, in most supermarkets.

Soybean, or soya bean, is the most significant of all beans. It has been cultivated by the Chinese for thousands of years and its byproducts are used in many forms, including the making of margarine and in non-food items such as soaps and plastics. It is inexpensive and nutrition-packed, and ranges in size from as small as a pea to as large as a cherry, in various combinations of red, yellow, green, brown, and black. The flavor is quite bland and soybeans can be cooked like any other dried bean or sprouted to be used in salads and as a cooked vegetable.

SOAKING AND COOKING METHODS

Before starting to prepare any dried legume, spread them out and sort through them for any foreign material such as small stones, grit, or bad beans. After sorting, put them in a colander and wash them well.

Fava beans may need to be shelled before soaking them. Put the unshelled fava beans in a pot and cover with water by three inches. Bring them to a boil and simmer for 10 minutes. Cover the pot and allow the beans to cool. Drain the beans thoroughly and remove the tough outer shells of the beans. (At this point they should practically pop out of their shells.) Soak the shelled fava beans for several hours or overnight before cooking.

Almost all dried legumes, except lentils and split peas, should be soaked for several hours or overnight before cooking them. Soaking dried beans and peas makes for faster and more even cooking and it dissolves some of the gas-causing, indigestible sugars so the legumes are more easily digested. After the legumes have been soaked, discard the soaking water and rinse with clean, fresh water before cooking them.

The overnight soaking method is by far the best method when time permits. Place the rinsed legumes in a large bowl. Add 10 cups of fresh water for each pound of dried legumes and allow them to soak for at least 8 hours or, preferably, overnight.

I have found that if you are going to soak beans or peas anyway, go ahead and soak twice as many as you need. Then drain and rinse the soaked legumes, use what you need, and freeze the rest for next time. That way you always have some available for easy convenience—all you have to do is thaw them out.

You can shorten the soaking time somewhat with the hot soak method. Place the rinsed legumes in a large pot. Add 10 cups of fresh water for each pound of dried legumes. Bring the water to a boil and boil for 2 to 3 minutes. Remove from the heat and allow to stand for at least 2 hours and, preferably, for 4 hours.

The quick soak method requires the least time of all. Proceed as you would for the hot soak method, but the legumes only stand for 1 hour after being boiled. It should be noted that legumes labeled "quick-cooking" have already been presoaked and then dried again, so they require no presoaking. They will not have the same texture as regular dried legumes, however.

COOKING LEGUMES

After the legumes have been soaked and rinsed, there are several approaches you can use to cook them. Cooking legumes in unsalted stock, instead of water, can add greatly to their flavor. You may also wish to add nonacidic seasonings, such as onion, garlic, pepper, and mustard during the cooking process. However, salt, baking soda, wine, vinegar, lemon juice, tomatoes, and molasses added to legumes before they are cooked can toughen the skins. Therefore, unless instructed otherwise in a recipe, do not add these or any acidic ingredients until the beans are already cooked.

The most familiar cooking method is on top of the stove in a pot. After the legumes have been soaked and rinsed, place them in the cooking pot and add fresh water (or stock) to cover by two inches. Bring to a boil over medium heat, then reduce the heat to low and cook, covered, until the legumes are tender. Cooking times will vary greatly depending upon the size of the legume, its age, and how long it was soaked.

Kidney beans, chick-peas, pinks, and navy beans will require about 1 to 1 ½ hours by the stove-top method. Limas, about 45 minutes to an hour, and black-eyed peas from 30 minutes to an hour. To check on the tenderness of the legume during the cooking process, remove a whole bean or pea from the cooking liquid and squeeze it between your fingers. It should crush easily, but with some resistance. It should not be mushy!

For slow cooking, nothing beats a Crockpot. To find out the best method, I went to my friend Mabel Hoffman. She is the author of *Crock Pot Cookery*, and the person I consider to be the leading authority on Crockpot cooking in the country. She told me that even when using a Crockpot it is always best to soak legumes for 8 hours or overnight before cooking them. However, it is possible to cook unsoaked legumes in a Crockpot—it just takes longer.

Mabel recommends cooking soaked legumes for 11 to 12 hours, and unsoaked legumes for 13 to 14 hours. She also suggests cooking legumes in the Crockpot on high for the first 2 hours and then on low for the remaining cooking time. Always check the directions supplied by the manufacturer of your particular Crockpot.

Though pressure cooking and microwave cooking are both great time-savers, they are not recommended for legumes. Loose skins can clog the steam vent of the pressure cooker, resulting in a dangerous buildup of pressure and possible explosion—messy, to say the least. And though the microwave is a wonderful way to reheat cooked legumes, it isn't very satisfactory for the initial cooking process—the inside of the legume turns to mush long before the outside becomes tender.

Due to the fact that canned beans come in a variety of can sizes, ranging from 15 to 16 ounces, I have standardized all recipes to call for 16-ounce cans. If you can only find 15-, 15 ¼-, or 15 ½-ounce cans, don't worry about it—they all work just fine in the recipes.

BASICS

※

FIFTEEN-MINUTE CHICKEN STOCK

※

Making your own stock is essential not only to good light cooking but for any kind of tasty cooking, whether it's healthy or not. You will notice in the recipe that the carrots are scraped and the leaves are removed from the celery, but that the onions and garlic do not have to be peeled. The reason for this is that the outside of the carrot has oxidized and therefore tends to add a bitter taste to the stock, as do the leaves of the celery. Any ingredient that adds a bitter taste should be avoided in any recipe. The onions do not need to be peeled because the onion skins do not affect the taste of the stock; in fact, brown onion skins add a little desirable color. After the chicken stock has cooked for an hour or more, you may want to throw in a whole chicken and cook it for your dinner or have it to dice for a salad or casserole the next day. It will take the chicken less than an hour to cook, and overcooking can make it tough and dry; so as soon as it is tender, remove it from the stockpot.

3 to 5 pounds chicken bones, parts, and giblets, excluding liver (buy chicken parts for stock from a butcher or save chicken carcasses in the freezer until ready to make stock)
2 carrots, scraped and chopped
2 ribs celery, without leaves, chopped
1 onion, unpeeled, quartered
3 parsley sprigs
2 to 4 cloves garlic, halved
1 bay leaf
12 black peppercorns
¼ cup vinegar
Cold water to cover

1. Put all the ingredients into a large pot with a lid. Add cold water to cover and bring slowly to a boil over medium heat. Preparation up to this point takes about 5 minutes.

2. Reduce the heat to low, cover, leaving the lid ajar, and simmer for 3 hours or more. Longer cooking makes the stock more flavorful. Remove from the heat and allow to stand until cool enough to handle. Remove the chicken parts and vegetables and discard. Strain the stock and cool to room temperature. This second step takes 5 minutes more. Refrigerate, uncovered, overnight or until the fat has congealed on top.

3. Remove the fat and store the stock in the freezer in containers of a volume you most often use. I like to freeze mine in ice cube trays and then store the cubes of stock in plastic freezer bags. Two cubes equals about ¼ cup stock. This step completes the 15 minutes of preparation time.

MAKES APPROXIMATELY 10 CUPS (2 ½ QUARTS)

Each cup contains negligible calories, cholesterol, and fat, and variable sodium.

Variation: Turkey Stock

Substitute 1 turkey carcass for chicken and use herbs and spices of your choice.

BEEF STOCK

Basically, beef stock is made exactly the same way you make chicken stock. The only difference is the first step, where you brown the bones and vegetables prior to starting the stock. The reason for browning the ingredients is to give a rich, dark color to the stock. Pale meat stocks do not make sauces and gravies look as rich and appetizing. Also, a foam or scum rises to the surface of a meat stock and must be removed at least once and sometimes several times when the stock first comes to a boil. Veal knuckles are ideal to use for the bones. The optional addition of the beef or veal makes for a richer stock.

3 pounds beef or veal bones
1 pound beef or veal, any cut (optional)
1 tomato, halved
3 carrots, scraped and chopped
2 ribs celery, without leaves, chopped
1 large onion unpeeled, quartered
3 parsley sprigs
3 cloves garlic, halved
¼ teaspoon dried thyme, crushed
¼ teaspoon dried marjoram, crushed
1 bay leaf
12 peppercorns
¼ cup vinegar
Cold water to cover

1. Place the bones, meat, and vegetables in a roasting pan in a 400°F oven until well browned, about 40 minutes, turning frequently to brown evenly.

2. Remove from the roasting pan and place in a large pot with a lid. Add all the other ingredients and cover with cold water by 1 inch. Bring slowly to a boil over medium heat. Simmer slowly for 5 minutes and remove any scum on the surface. Reduce the heat to low, cover, leaving the lid ajar, and simmer for 2 to 6 hours. Cooking longer makes the stock more flavorful.

3. Remove from the heat and allow to stand until cool enough to handle. Remove the bones, meat, and vegetables and discard. Strain the stock and cool to room temperature.

4. Refrigerate, uncovered, overnight or until the fat has congealed on top. Remove the fat and store the stock in the freezer in the size containers you most often use.

MAKES APPROXIMATELY 10 CUPS (2 ½ QUARTS)

Each cup contains negligible calories, cholesterol, and fat, and variable sodium.

SOUTHERN "SEASONING"

This recipe for southern seasoning was sent to me by a reader. I tried it immediately and have been using it ever since to make Baked Beans, page 214, and Red Beans and Brown Rice, page 215. It is a great and very low-fat flavor-enhancer for many other bean dishes, soups, stews, and sauces.

1 to 2 pounds ham hocks or smoked pork hocks
8 to 10 cups water, or to cover

1. Put the ham hocks in a deep pot or soup kettle, cover with water, and bring to a boil. Reduce the heat to low and cook, covered, until the meat starts to fall off of the bones, about 3 hours.

2. Cool to room temperature and then refrigerate, uncovered, overnight. Remove all fat congealed on the top and remove the ham hocks from the liquid and discard the bones, skin, and all fat. Shred the lean meat, return it to the liquid, and mix well.

3. Spoon the mixture into ice cube trays and freeze. When frozen, pop the cubes of "seasoning" from the trays and store in plastic freezer bags. Use the frozen cubes to season soups, stews, and casseroles. Two cubes equal about ¼ cup.

MAKES ABOUT 6 CUPS STOCK, TWENTY-FOUR ¼-CUP SERVINGS

Each serving contains approximately 15 calories; 3 mg cholesterol;
negligible fat; 110 mg sodium.

FISH STOCK

There is nothing better than a good fish stock for poaching fish and seafood, or for making a rich fish soup or stew. I also like to use fish stock to moisten the pan for sautéing or braising fish or seafood. When fish heads are not available, I often make a shellfish stock using shrimp, crab, or lobster shells.

> 3 quarts water
> ¼ cup vinegar
> 2 pounds fish heads, bones, and trimmings
> 2 onions, sliced
> 5 parsley sprigs
> 1 carrot, scraped and chopped
> ½ teaspoon dried marjoram, crushed
> ¼ teaspoon black peppercorns
> ½ teaspoon salt
> 1 tablespoon fresh lemon juice

Bring all the ingredients to a boil and simmer for 40 minutes. Line a strainer with damp cheesecloth and strain the stock through it, discarding the bones and vegetables. Cool to room temperature. Refrigerate. Freeze the stock not needed immediately, using the size containers that will most nearly fit your requirements.

MAKES ABOUT 2 QUARTS

1 cup contains negligible calories, cholesterol, and fat, and variable sodium.

COURT BOUILLON

Court bouillon is actually a fancy name for seasoned water and is used as a substitute for fish stock for poaching fish and seafood. I much prefer using fish stock or even chicken stock for cooking fish or seafood, but you don't always have it on hand when you need it. Court bouillon is certainly a better substitute than just plain water!

> 6 *cups water*
> ⅓ *cup white vinegar*
> 1 *lemon, including peel, sliced*
> 2 *ribs celery, without leaves, sliced*
> 2 *carrots, scraped and sliced*
> 1 *onion, sliced*
> 2 *whole cloves garlic, peeled*
> 2 *bay leaves*
> 12 *black peppercorns*

1. Combine all the ingredients in a large pot and bring to a boil. Reduce the heat and simmer, uncovered, for 45 minutes.

2. Strain through two layers of damp cheesecloth and store in the freezer in the size containers you will require.

3. Use for cooking shrimp, crab, or lobster or to poach any fish. This court bouillon may be used and refrozen many times, straining after each use.

MAKES 6 CUPS

Each cup contains negligible calories, cholesterol, and fat, and variable sodium.

VEGETABLE STOCK

Vegetable stock is an essential ingredient for running a purely vegetarian kitchen where chicken, beef, and fish stocks cannot be used. Basically you can make vegetable stock from almost any combination of vegetables as long as you eliminate any ingredient that might add bitterness, such as carrot peelings or celery leaves. Try my recipe and then experiment with your own favorite vegetables. Use your imagination and your leftover vegetables and you can create lots of your own vegetable stock recipes in which to poach, steam, or sauté all of your favorite foods.

1 pound cabbage, shredded (4 cups)
2 pounds onions, chopped (6 cups)
1 pound carrots, scraped and chopped (4 cups)
2 pounds celery, without leaves, chopped (6 cups)
¼ pound fresh parsley, chopped (2 cups)
2 bay leaves
2 teaspoons dried marjoram, crushed
1 teaspoon salt
1 gallon water

1. Combine all the ingredients in a large pot and bring to a boil. Reduce the heat and simmer for 1 hour, covered.

2. Strain and refrigerate the stock in a tightly covered container, or store in the freezer in the size containers most used for individual recipes. Freeze some stock in ice cube trays to use in sautéeing. Discard the vegetables or puree them as a side dish.

MAKES APPROXIMATELY 3 QUARTS

Each cup contains negligible calories, no cholesterol, negligible fat, and variable sodium.

WHITE SAUCE

This version of a classic approach to white or béchamel sauce is exceptionally easy and is much lower in fat than the traditional recipes. It is also practically cholesterol-free and works well as a base for any recipe calling for a creamy type sauce.

1 tablespoon corn-oil margarine
3 tablespoons sifted unbleached all-purpose flour
2 ½ cups nonfat milk, heated to simmering
⅛ teaspoon salt

1. Melt the margarine over low heat. Add the flour and cook for 2 minutes, stirring constantly. Do not brown.

2. Remove from the heat and add the milk slowly, stirring constantly with a wire whisk. Add the salt and cook slowly for about 20 minutes, stirring occasionally. (If you wish a thicker sauce, cook it a little longer.)

MAKES 2 CUPS, EIGHT ¼-CUP SERVINGS

Each serving contains approximately 50 calories; 1 mg cholesterol; 2 g fat; 75 mg sodium.

Variation: Mornay Sauce

When the sauce has thickened, add ⅛ teaspoon ground white pepper, ⅛ teaspoon freshly grated nutmeg, and ½ cup grated Swiss or Gruyère cheese (2 ounces). For a thinner sauce, add more nonfat milk.

LEMON SAUCE

I like to serve this sauce with the Black Bean Strudel on page 122. It is also good served with fish or poultry.

1 tablespoon cornstarch
1 cup low-fat (2%) milk
3 tablespoons fresh lemon juice
1 large egg plus 1 egg white, lightly beaten
1 teaspoon olive oil
1 teaspoon grated lemon zest, yellow part only
¼ teaspoon sweet paprika

¼ teaspoon ground white pepper
⅛ teaspoon turmeric for color (optional)

Dissolve the cornstarch in the milk. Combine with the remaining ingredients in the top of a double boiler. Cook, stirring constantly, over medium-high heat until the sauce is the consistency of a soft mayonnaise, 10 to 12 minutes. May be served hot or cold.

MAKES EIGHT 2-TABLESPOON SERVINGS

Each serving contains approximately 38 calories; 29 mg cholesterol; 2 g fat; 30 mg sodium.

MEXICAN SALSA

When working with hot peppers, be sure never to touch your face or eyes. If your skin is sensitive, wearing rubber gloves is recommended.

3 medium, ripe tomatoes, finely diced (2 cups)
½ medium onion, finely diced (¾ cup)
2 tablespoons finely chopped cilantro (fresh coriander)
½ jalapeño pepper, seeded and finely chopped, or to taste
½ clove garlic, finely chopped, or to taste
¾ teaspoon ground cumin
⅛ teaspoon salt
1 tablespoon fresh lemon juice
1 tablespoon fresh lime juice

Combine all the ingredients, cover, and refrigerate for at least 2 hours before serving.

MAKES 1 ½ CUPS, SIX ¼-CUP SERVINGS

Each serving contains approximately 15 calories; no cholesterol; negligible fat; 40 mg sodium.

MARINARA SAUCE

This is the easiest-to-make, best-tasting, and lowest-calorie marinara sauce you have ever eaten. It is wonderful on any pasta and is also delicious on fish, poultry, and meat dishes.

> *5 cups prepared tomato sauce*
> *2 ½ cups water*
> *2 medium onions, finely chopped (3 cups)*
> *2 cloves garlic, finely chopped (2 teaspoons)*
> *1 teaspoon dried oregano, crushed*
> *1 teaspoon dried basil, crushed*
> *¼ teaspoon dried rosemary, crushed*
> *¼ teaspoon dried thyme, crushed*
> *1 bay leaf, broken*
> *⅛ teaspoon freshly ground black pepper*
> *½ teaspoon salt*
> *½ teaspoon fructose or ¾ teaspoon sugar*

1. Combine all the ingredients and bring to a boil. Reduce the heat and simmer, covered, for at least 2 hours.

2. Cool to room temperature and refrigerate or freeze in containers of appropriate size.

MAKES 4 CUPS

½ cup contains approximately 70 calories; no cholesterol; 5g fat; 1060 mg sodium.

MANDARIN DRESSING AND MARINADE

This dressing and marinade also works perfectly for wok cooking and adds enormously to the flavor of stir-fries of all types.

½ *cup rice wine vinegar*

3 tablespoons dark sesame oil

1 tablespoon reduced-sodium soy sauce

One 6-ounce can (¾ cup) frozen unsweetened pineapple juice concentrate, undiluted

2 teaspoons chopped peeled fresh ginger

1 clove garlic, chopped

⅛ *teaspoon red pepper flakes*

Combine all the ingredients in a blender container and mix well. Refrigerate in a tightly covered container. Mix well before each use.

MAKES 1 ½ CUPS, TWELVE 2-TABLESPOON SERVINGS

Each serving contains approximately 65 calories; no cholesterol; 3 g fat; 85 mg sodium.

CAJUN SPICE MIX

1 tablespoon paprika

2 ½ teaspoons salt

1 teaspoon onion powder

1 teaspoon garlic powder

1 teaspoon ground cayenne pepper

¾ *teaspoon ground white pepper*

¾ *teaspoon freshly ground black pepper*

½ *teaspoon dried oregano, crushed*

½ *teaspoon dried thyme, crushed*

Combine all the spices and mix until well blended. Store, tightly covered, in a cool, dry place.

MAKES 3 ½ TABLESPOONS, TWENTY-ONE ½-TEASPOON SERVINGS

Each serving contains approximately 3 calories; no cholesterol; negligible fat; 250 mg sodium.

SOUPS

MACARONI AND CHEDDAR SOUP

4 tablespoons (½ stick) corn-oil margarine
½ cup unbleached all-purpose flour
2 cups defatted chicken stock (see page 15)
2 cups nonfat milk
1 teaspoon salt (omit if using salted stock)
⅛ teaspoon ground white pepper
8 ounces reduced-fat mild Cheddar cheese, shredded (2 cups)
1 medium carrot, scraped and finely diced (½ cup)
1 medium rib celery, finely diced (½ cup)
1 small onion, finely diced (¾ cup)
1 cup elbow macaroni or small shells, cooked al dente (2 ½ cups)
½ cup frozen corn
½ cup frozen peas

1. Melt 3 tablespoons of the margarine in a large saucepan. Add the flour and stir over medium heat for 1 minute; do not brown. Add the stock and milk and, using a wire whisk, stir the mixture over medium heat until it comes to a boil, about 20 minutes. Add the salt, white pepper, and cheese, and stir until the cheese is melted. Cover and set aside.

2. Melt the remaining tablespoon of margarine in another saucepan over low heat. Cook, the carrot, celery, and onion until the onion is soft and translucent, about 10 minutes. Add the onion mixture to the cheese soup mixture along with the macaroni, corn, and peas and cook and stir just until heated to the desired serving temperature.

MAKES 7 CUPS, 6 SERVINGS

Each serving contains approximately 385 calories; 34 mg cholesterol; 18 g fat; 714 mg sodium.

EGGPLANT AND ORZO SOUP WITH ROASTED RED PEPPERS

This recipe can easily be turned into a delicious sauce for your favorite pasta. Omit the orzo and, right after the addition of the vinegar, puree all the ingredients in a food processor until smooth.

2 large red bell peppers
2 large eggplants (4 pounds)
1 large onion, finely chopped (2 cups)
2 cloves garlic, pressed or minced
4 cups defatted chicken stock (see page 15)
½ teaspoon salt (omit if using salted stock)
1 teaspoon freshly ground black pepper
½ teaspoon balsamic vinegar
2 cups cooked orzo
6 sprigs fresh thyme, for garnish (optional)

1. Preheat the oven to 425°F. Spray a baking sheet with nonstick vegetable coating. Halve the bell peppers, lengthwise, and remove the seeds and membranes. Place the peppers, cut side down, on the baking sheet. Halve the eggplants, lengthwise and place them, cut side down, on the same baking sheet. Bake until the skins are wrinkled and slightly charred, about 15 to 20 minutes.

2. Remove the vegetables from the oven and allow them to cool until safe to handle. Cut the peppers into thin strips and remove the skins. Set the peeled pepper strips aside. Peel the eggplant and carefully remove and discard the seeds. Finely chop the flesh and set it aside.

3. Combine the onion and garlic in a saucepan or soup kettle and cook, covered, over low heat until the onion is soft and translucent, 10 to 15 minutes. Stir occasionally and add a little water or stock, if necessary, to prevent scorching. Add the chopped eggplant, stock, salt, and pepper and cook, covered, for 15 minutes. Add the vinegar and mix well.

4. To serve, place ⅓ cup of the cooked pasta into each of six bowls. Divide the roasted red pepper strips among each serving and ladle 1 cup of soup over the top. Garnish with sprigs of fresh thyme, if desired.

MAKES 6 SERVINGS

Each serving contains approximately 184 calories; no cholesterol; 1 g fat;
522 mg sodium.

MINESTRONE

1 large onion, finely chopped (2 cups)
2 cloves garlic, pressed or minced
2 medium carrots, scraped and cut into ¼-inch rounds
One 14 ½-ounce can ready-cut tomatoes, undrained
2 cups defatted chicken stock (see page 15)
½ teaspoon dried oregano, crushed
½ teaspoon dried marjoram, crushed
½ teaspoon dried basil, crushed
¼ teaspoon freshly ground black pepper
½ cup small elbow macaroni
One 16-ounce can kidney beans, undrained
8 ounces fresh spinach, stems and large veins removed and cut into thin
   strips
¼ cup packed chopped fresh parsley
Freshly grated Parmesan cheese

1. Combine the onion, garlic, and carrots in a large pot or soup kettle and cook, covered, over low heat until the onion is soft and translucent, 10 to 15 minutes. Stir occasionally and add a little water or stock, if necessary, to prevent scorching.

2. Add the tomatoes plus their juice, the stock, oregano, marjoram, basil, and pepper and bring to a boil over medium-high heat. Add the macaroni and cook until the macaroni is tender, about 10 minutes. Add the beans and the liquid from the can, the spinach and parsley and cook until heated through, about 5 more minutes. Serve freshly grated Parmesan cheese on the side to sprinkle on the top, if desired.

MAKES ABOUT 7 CUPS, FOUR 1 ¾-CUP SERVINGS

*Each serving contains approximately 536 calories; 0 mg cholesterol; 2 g fat;
477 mg sodium.*

SEAFOOD PASTA CHOWDER

2 tablespoons corn-oil margarine
½ pound fresh mushrooms sliced (3 cups)
Two 1-ounce packets Knorr's Newburg Sauce Mix
3 cups low-fat milk
1 ½ cups water
¼ cup dry white wine
¼ cup sliced scallions
6 ounces miniature shells or bow-tie pasta, al dente and drained (4 cups)
3 ounces cooked crabmeat, sorted to remove any shell pieces
Cropped fresh parsley, for garnish

1. Melt the margarine in a 3-quart nonreactive saucepan. Add the mushrooms and cook and stir for 3 minutes over medium-high heat. Add the sauce mix and mix well. Add the milk, water, and wine and stir constantly with a wire whisk until the mixture comes to a boil. Reduce the heat to low and simmer 8 minutes, stirring constantly.

2. Add the scallions, pasta, and crabmeat to the sauce mixture. Stir to heat through and spoon into serving bowls. Garnish with parsley.

MAKES 7 ½ CUPS, SIX 1 ¼-CUP SERVINGS

Each serving contains approximately 259 calories; 17 mg cholesterol; 9 g fat; 325 mg sodium.

FISH SOUP WITH PASTA SHELLS

1 small onion, finely chopped (1 cup)
2 cloves garlic
½ cup dry vermouth
One 8-ounce bottle clam juice
One 28-ounce can ready-cut tomatoes, undrained
1 cup water
4 ounces pasta shells
3 small zucchini, cut into ½-inch rounds (3 cups)
1 cup fresh or frozen corn kernels
½ teaspoon salt
¼ teaspoon freshly ground black pepper
½ teaspoon dried oregano, crushed
½ teaspoon dried basil, crushed
½ teaspoon dried thyme, crushed
¼ teaspoon dried rosemary, crushed
1 ½ pounds fresh firm white fish, cubed

1. Combine the onion and garlic in a large heavy pot or soup kettle. Cook, covered, over low heat until soft and translucent, 10 to 15 minutes. Stir occasionally and add a little water or stock, if necessary, to prevent scorching.

2. Add the vermouth and cook, stirring constantly, until almost dry. Add the clam juice, tomatoes and their juice, water, and pasta shells. Bring to a boil over medium-high heat, then reduce the heat and simmer, uncovered, for 15 minutes.

3. Add all remaining ingredients, except the fish, and simmer for 6 minutes. Add the fish and cook just until the fish turns from translucent to opaque—about 4 minutes.

MAKES ABOUT 10 CUPS, SIX 1 ½-CUP SERVINGS

Each serving contains approximately 257 calories; 50 mg cholesterol; 2 g fat; 560 mg sodium.

SPAGHETTI AND LENTIL SOUP

1 tablespoon olive oil
4 ounces Canadian bacon, diced
1 medium onion, chopped (1 ½ cups)
3 cloves garlic, pressed or minced
4 Roma tomatoes, peeled and diced (2 cups)
1 cup dry lentils
4 cups water or defatted chicken stock (see page 15)
¼ teaspoon freshly ground black pepper
½ teaspoon salt (omit if using salted stock)
½ cup broken spaghetti
Chopped fresh parsley, for garnish (optional)
Freshly grated Parmesan cheese, for garnish (optional)

1. Heat the oil in a saucepan. Add the bacon, onion, and garlic and cook over medium-low heat, stirring frequently, until the onion is soft and translucent, 10 to 15 minutes.

2. Add the tomatoes and lentils and mix well. Add the water or stock and the pepper and bring to a boil over medium-high heat. Reduce the heat to low and simmer, uncovered, until the lentils are tender, but not mushy, 30 to 40 minutes. Add the salt and spaghetti and cook for 10 more minutes.

3. Serve hot and garnish with chopped parsley and Parmesan cheese, if desired.

MAKES ABOUT 7 ½ CUPS, SIX 1 ¼-CUP SERVINGS

Each serving contains approximately 228 calories; 11 mg cholesterol; 5 g fat; 818 mg sodium.

FRESH ASPARAGUS AND RICE SOUP

1 tablespoon extra virgin olive oil
½ cup chopped onion
1 pound fresh asparagus
¼ teaspoon salt
⅛ teaspoon freshly ground black pepper
¼ teaspoon dried basil, crushed
2 cups defatted chicken stock (see page 15)
8 fresh spinach leaves, stems removed, and blanched
1 cup cooked brown rice

1. Warm the oil in a saucepan over medium heat. Add the onion and cook, stirring occasionally, until the onion is soft and translucent, 10 to 15 minutes.

2. Break the tough ends off of the asparagus spears and cut the spears in 1-inch pieces. (You should have about 2 cups chopped asparagus.)

3. Add the asparagus to the onion and cook, stirring frequently, about 5 minutes. Add the salt, pepper, basil, and stock and bring to a boil. Reduce the heat to low and simmer, covered, for 10 minutes.

4. Spoon the mixture into a blender container and blend until smooth, leaving the lid ajar to allow the hot steam to escape. Add the blanched spinach leaves, for color, and again blend until smooth. Pour the mixture through a strainer, pressing the liquid through with the back of a large spoon.

5. Add the rice to the soup and serve. If desired the soup may be reheated before serving, served at room temperature, or refrigerated, covered, and served cold.

MAKES ABOUT 4 CUPS, FOUR 1-CUP SERVINGS

Each serving contains approximately 172 calories; no cholesterol; 5 g fat; 486 mg sodium.

WILD RICE AND BARLEY SOUP

½ cup wild rice, washed and drained
½ cup pearl barley, washed and drained
1 ½ teaspoons cumin seeds
7 cups water or vegetable stock (see page 20)
2 carrots, scraped and diced (1 cup)
2 cups diced fennel, including the fern
2 Roma tomatoes, diced
1 ½ teaspoons finely chopped peeled fresh ginger root
1 serrano chile, seeded and finely chopped
1 teaspoon turmeric
1 ½ teaspoons ground coriander
1 teaspoon salt
2 tablespoons packed chopped cilantro (fresh coriander)

1. Combine the rice and barley in a bowl. Add hot water to cover and allow to soak for 2 hours. Drain well.

2. In a dry skillet over medium heat, toast the cumin seeds until aromatic. Set aside.

3. In a large pot or soup kettle, combine the wild rice, barley, cumin seeds, and all remaining ingredients except the salt and cilantro. Bring to a boil over medium heat. Reduce the heat to low and simmer, covered, until the rice is tender, about 45 minutes. Remove from the heat and stir in the salt and cilantro, mixing well.

MAKES 12 CUPS, EIGHT 1 ½-CUP SERVINGS

Each serving contains approximately 143 calories; no cholesterol; 2 g fat; 1940 mg sodium.

WILD RICE AND CABBAGE SOUP

3 ½ cups defatted chicken stock (see page 15)
½ cup wild rice
½ teaspoon caraway seeds
¼ teaspoon fennel seeds
½ teaspoon freshly ground black pepper
½ head cabbage, chopped
½ teaspoon salt (omit if using salted stock)

1. Bring 1 ½ cups of the stock to a boil in a saucepan over medium-high heat. Add the wild rice, caraway seeds, fennel seeds, and pepper. Mix well and bring back to a boil. Reduce the heat to low and cook, covered, until the rice kernels burst and are tender, about 45 minutes.

2. Combine the remaining 2 cups of stock, the cabbage, and salt in a large saucepan. Bring to a boil over medium-high heat. Reduce the heat to low and simmer, covered, for 10 minutes. Add the cooked rice and mix well.

MAKES 4 CUPS, FOUR 1-CUP SERVINGS

Each serving contains approximately 111 calories; no cholesterol; 1 g fat; 376 mg sodium.

CHICKEN AND WILD RICE SOUP

2 tablespoons diced onion
½ clove garlic, pressed or minced
2 cups defatted chicken stock (see page 15)
2 tablespoons diced carrot
2 tablespoons diced celery
1 teaspoon packed chopped fresh basil
½ teaspoon dried oregano, crushed
¼ teaspoon salt (omit if using salted stock)
⅛ teaspoon freshly ground black pepper
1 cup cooked wild rice
1 cup diced cooked boneless, skinless chicken
3 tablespoons julienne-cut escarole
2 teaspoons freshly grated Romano cheese

1. In a medium-size saucepan, combine the onion and garlic and cook, covered, over low heat until soft, 5 to 10 minutes. Stir occasionally and add a little water or stock, if necessary, to prevent scorching.

2. Add the stock, carrot, celery, basil, oregano, salt, and pepper and bring to a boil over medium heat. Reduce the heat to low and simmer, covered, until the vegetables are tender, about 15 minutes.

3. Just before serving, stir in the rice, chicken, escarole, and Romano cheese and heat through.

MAKES 4 CUPS, FOUR 1-CUP SERVINGS

Each serving contains approximately 112 calories; 25 mg cholesterol; 2 g fat; 670 mg sodium.

RAPID RICE AND TURKEY SOUP

1 medium onion, finely chopped (1 ½ cups)
1 clove garlic, pressed
2 medium carrots, scraped and grated
½ pound fresh mushrooms, sliced (2 cups)
1 rib celery, without leaves, finely chopped
4 cups defatted chicken stock (see page 15)
½ teaspoon salt (omit if using salted stock)
¼ teaspoon freshly ground black pepper
2 cups cooked brown rice
2 cups diced cooked turkey, without the skin
2 tablespoons chopped fresh parsley
2 tablespoons chopped fresh chives

1. Combine the onion and garlic in a heavy pot or soup kettle over low heat and cook, covered, until soft and translucent, 10 to 15 minutes. Stir occasionally and add a little water or stock, if necessary, to prevent scorching. Add the carrots, mushrooms, and celery, and cook, stirring frequently, until the vegetables are tender.

2. Add the stock, salt, and pepper and bring to a boil over medium-high heat. Add all remaining ingredients, return to a boil, and remove from the heat.

MAKES SIX 1 ⅓-CUP SERVINGS

Each serving contains approximately 210 calories; 30 mg cholesterol; 3 g fat; 694 mg sodium.

HOMEMADE WILD RICE SOUP

1 tablespoon corn-oil margarine
¼ pound Canadian bacon, cut into ½-inch pieces
½ pound fresh mushrooms, sliced (2 cups)
1 large onion, chopped (2 cups)
1 clove garlic, minced
2 tablespoons unbleached all-purpose flour
2 cups low-fat milk
1 ½ cups defatted chicken stock (see page 15)
1 ¼ pounds potatoes, peeled, boiled, and diced (3 cups)
4 cups cooked wild rice (1 cup uncooked)
½ teaspoon salt (omit if using salted stock)
¼ teaspoon ground white pepper
4 ounces fat-reduced sharp Cheddar cheese, grated

1. Melt the margarine over medium heat in a large kettle. Add the bacon, mushrooms, onion, and garlic and cook until the onion is soft, about 10 minutes. Add the flour and cook, stirring, for 1 minute. Slowly pour in the milk and stock. Cook, stirring occasionally, until the soup is slightly thickened, about 15 minutes.

2. Combine 1 cup of the diced potatoes with several tablespoons of the soup liquid in a blender and blend until smooth. Pour back into the soup and stir in the remaining potatoes, the rice, salt, and white pepper. Add the grated cheese a little at a time until all the cheese is melted and the soup is warmed through.

MAKES ABOUT 10 CUPS, EIGHT 1 ¼-CUP SERVINGS

Each serving contains approximately 339 calories; 22 mg cholesterol; 11 g fat; 1035 mg sodium.

SPLIT MUNG DAL

¾ cup dried split mung beans, without skins
6 cups water
1 serrano chile, seeded and finely chopped
2 teaspoons finely chopped peeled fresh ginger
½ teaspoon turmeric
1 teaspoon ground coriander
1 tablespoon peanut oil
1 ½ teaspoons cumin seeds
2 cloves garlic, pressed or minced
1 teaspoon salt
2 tablespoons packed chopped cilantro (fresh coriander)

1. Wash and drain the beans. In a heavy pot, combine the beans, water, chile, ginger, turmeric, and coriander. Bring to a boil over medium heat. Reduce the heat to low and cook, covered, until the beans are tender, about 1 hour.

2. Warm the oil in a small skillet over medium heat. Add the cumin seeds and stir-fry until they turn brown and aromatic. Add the garlic and cook, stirring constantly, for 1 more minute. Add the garlic mixture to the soup and remove the soup from the heat. Stir in the salt and allow the soup to rest for 5 minutes. Just before serving, stir in the cilantro.

MAKES ABOUT 6 CUPS, SIX 1-CUP SERVINGS

Each serving contains approximately 115 calories; no cholesterol; 3 g fat; 397 mg sodium.

INDIAN SWEET CHICK-PEA SOUP

1 cup small dried chick-peas, soaked overnight in water to cover
8 cups water
2 bay leaves
5 Roma tomatoes, diced (3 cups)
1 tablespoon canola oil
½ teaspoon cumin seeds
1 teaspoon grated peeled fresh ginger
2 cloves garlic, pressed or minced
2 tablespoons firmly packed dark brown sugar
2 tablespoons molasses
1 teaspoon salt

1. Drain and rinse the chick-peas. In a heavy pot, combine the drained chick-peas and water and bring to a boil over medium heat. Remove any foam that forms on the top. Add the bay leaves, reduce the heat to low, and simmer, covered, until the chick-peas are tender, about 40 minutes. Add the tomatoes and continue to cook, uncovered, for 15 more minutes.

2. While the mixture is cooking, warm the oil in a small skillet over medium heat. Add the cumin seeds and stir-fry until aromatic. Add the ginger and garlic and stir-fry for 1 more minute. Add the garlic mixture to the chick-peas and mix well. Stir in the brown sugar, molasses, and salt, and cook for 5 more minutes. Serve hot.

MAKES ABOUT 8 CUPS, EIGHT 1-CUP SERVINGS

Each serving contains approximately 145 calories; no cholesterol; 3 g fat; 310 mg sodium.

EASY EGGPLANT AND BEAN SOUP

1 medium onion, chopped (1 ½ cups)
1 clove garlic, pressed or minced
1 small red bell pepper, seeded and diced (¾ cup)
½ teaspoon ground coriander
½ teaspoon ground cumin
1 teaspoon chili powder
4 cups peeled and diced eggplant (about 1 pound)
One 28-ounce can ready-cut tomatoes, undrained
One 16-ounce can kidney beans, undrained
1 teaspoon balsamic vinegar

1. Combine the onion, garlic, and bell pepper in a large heavy pot or soup kettle. Cook, covered, over low heat until soft, 10 to 15 minutes. Stir occasionally and add a little water or stock, if necessary, to prevent scorching.

2. Add the coriander, cumin, chili powder, and eggplant. Mix well and cook, covered, for 10 more minutes. Add the tomatoes and their juice and the beans and their juice, and continue to cook, covered, for 20 minutes more. Add the balsamic vinegar and mix well. Serve hot.

MAKES ABOUT 6 CUPS, FOUR 1 ½-CUP SERVINGS

Each serving contains approximately 145 calories; no cholesterol; 3 g fat; 310 mg sodium.

BOMBAY MUNG BEAN AND YOGURT SOUP

4 cups water
4 cloves garlic
1 cup dried mung beans, rinsed, drained, and sorted
1 cup plain nonfat yogurt
1 teaspoon salt
¼ teaspoon ground coriander
¼ teaspoon ground cumin
¼ teaspoon turmeric
⅛ teaspoon ground cayenne pepper or to taste
3 cups cooked brown rice, at serving temperature

1. Bring 3 cups of the water to a boil in a 2 ½-quart saucepan. Cut two of the garlic cloves in half and add them to the water. Set the remaining garlic aside for later use. Add the drained beans and simmer over medium-low heat, stirring frequently, until the beans are tender, about 30 minutes.

2. Combine the yogurt and remaining cup of water in a bowl and mix well with a wire whisk or fork. Add the mixture to the beans and continue to simmer for another 30 minutes, stirring frequently.

3. Press or mince the reserved garlic. Combine the garlic with the remaining ingredients except the rice and mix well. Add the garlic mixture to the beans, mix well, and simmer for 10 more minutes. To serve, place ½ cup brown rice in each of six soup bowls or plates and ladle 1 cup of the hot soup over the top of each serving.

MAKES 6 SERVINGS

Each serving contains approximately 242 calories; negligible cholesterol; 1 g fat; 427 mg sodium.

NAVY BEAN SOUP

1 cup dried navy beans, soaked overnight in water to cover
1 bay leaf
4 cloves
5 cloves garlic
1 tablespoon olive oil
1 medium onion, finely chopped (1 ½ cups)
2 ribs celery, without leaves, finely chopped (1 cup)
3 medium carrots, scraped and diced (1 ½ cups)
¼ cup packed chopped fresh parsley
2 cups defatted chicken stock (see page 15)
2 tablespoons reduced-sodium soy sauce
¼ teaspoon freshly ground black pepper
⅛ teaspoon ground nutmeg

1. Drain, rinse, and pick over the beans. Place the beans in a medium-size saucepan. Add the bay leaf. Stick 2 cloves in each of 2 of the whole garlic cloves and add them to the pot. Add water to cover by 2 inches and bring to a boil over medium heat. Boil for 10 minutes, uncovered, then reduce the heat to low and simmer, covered, until the beans are tender, about 1 ½ hours.

2. While the beans are cooking, press or mince the remaining garlic and put it in a large pot or soup kettle. Add the olive oil and cook over low heat just until the garlic starts to sizzle. Add the onion, celery, carrots, and parsley and cook, covered, over low heat until the onion is soft and translucent, 10 to 15 minutes. Stir occasionally and add a little water or stock, if necessary, to prevent scorching.

3. Add the stock, soy sauce, pepper, and nutmeg to the vegetable mixture and simmer for 10 more minutes. Add the cooked beans and simmer 10 more minutes.

MAKES ABOUT 6 CUPS, SIX 1-CUP SERVINGS

Each serving contains approximately 232 calories; no cholesterol; 4 g fat;
610 mg sodium.

CHICK-PEA AND LENTIL SOUP

8 ounces dried chick-peas, soaked overnight in water to cover

8 ounces dried lentils, soaked overnight in water to cover

1 tablespoon extra virgin olive oil

½ medium onion, finely chopped (¾ cup)

6 cloves garlic, pressed or minced

6 cups defatted chicken stock (see page 15)

2 bay leaves

½ teaspoon salt (omit if using salted stock)

¼ teaspoon ground white pepper

2 ribs celery, diced (1 cup)

1 carrot, scraped and diced (½ cup)

1 cup diced white cabbage

1 small Japanese eggplant, diced

2 Roma tomatoes, peeled and diced

3 tablespoons fresh lemon juice

3 tablespoons white wine vinegar

Greek olives, for garnish (optional)

1. Drain the chick-peas and lentils. Set aside. Warm the oil in a large pot or soup kettle over medium heat. Add the onion and garlic and cook, stirring frequently, until soft and translucent, about 10 minutes. Add the chick-peas, stock, bay leaves, salt, and pepper. Mix well and bring to a boil. Reduce the heat to low and cook, covered, for 30 minutes. Add the lentils and continue to cook, covered, for 20 minutes more.

2. Remove half of the soup mixture from the pot and set aside. Puree the remaining soup in a blender or food processor until smooth, leaving the lid ajar for the hot steam to escape. Return the pureed mixture back to the pot.

3. Add the celery, carrot, cabbage, and eggplant to the pureed mixture and cook over medium heat, stirring frequently, for 10 minutes. Add the tomatoes, lemon juice, and vinegar to the reserved soup

mixture and cook, stirring frequently, until heated through, about 10 more minutes.

4. To serve, spoon 1 cup of hot soup into each of 12 bowls. Garnish with olives, if desired.

MAKES 12 CUPS, TWELVE 1-CUP SERVINGS

Each serving contains approximately 206 calories; no cholesterol; 3 g fat; 482 mg sodium.

BLACK-EYED PEA SOUP WITH TURNIPS AND GREENS

This soup is excellent served with corn bread for a hearty southern treat.

> 1 cup dried black-eyed peas, soaked overnight in water to cover
> 1 medium onion, finely chopped (1 ½ cups)
> 2 cloves garlic, pressed or minced
> 1 pound turnips, peeled and diced (3 cups)
> 1 carrot, scraped and diced
> 1 teaspoon dried thyme, crushed
> ½ teaspoon dried basil, crushed
> ½ teaspoon freshly ground black pepper
> 3 ½ cups defatted chicken stock (see page 15)
> 6 ounces turnip greens (or mustard greens, collard greens, kale, or spinach), thoroughly washed, stems removed and cut into thin strips
> ½ teaspoon salt (omit if using salted stock)

1. Rinse, drain, and pick over the peas. Combine the onion and garlic in a heavy pan or soup kettle and cook, covered, over low heat until soft and translucent, 10 to 15 minutes. Add the turnips, carrot, thyme, basil, and pepper and cook for 5 more minutes.

2. Add the stock to the onion mixture and bring to a boil over medium heat. Reduce the heat to low and cook, covered, until the peas are tender, about 1 hour. Stir in the greens and salt and cook for 5 more minutes.

MAKES ABOUT 6 CUPS, FOUR 1 ½-CUP SERVINGS

Each serving contains approximately 142 calories; no cholesterol; 1 g fat; 949 mg sodium.

BLACK BEAN BISQUE WITH CRAB

1 tablespoon olive oil
1 clove garlic, pressed or minced
½ cup minced onion
3 cups defatted chicken stock (see page 15)
One 16-ounce can black beans, undrained
⅛ teaspoon freshly ground black pepper
One 6-ounce can crabmeat, drained
2 tablespoons brandy
Chopped fresh chives, for garnish (optional)

1. Warm the oil in a saucepan over medium heat. Add the garlic and cook just until it starts to sizzle. Add the onion and cook, stirring occasionally, until soft and translucent, 10 to 15 minutes. Add the stock, the beans and their liquid, and the pepper. Reduce the heat and simmer, uncovered, for 30 minutes.

2. Pour the mixture into a blender container. Place the lid on the container, leaving it ajar for the hot steam to escape, and blend on high until smooth. Pour through a strainer, pressing the liquid through with the back of a large spoon.

3. Pour the strained liquid back into the saucepan, add the crab-meat and brandy and mix well. Bring to the desired temperature over medium-low heat before serving. Garnish with chopped chives, if desired.

MAKES ABOUT 4 CUPS, EIGHT ½-CUP SERVINGS

Each serving contains approximately 145 calories; 30 mg cholesterol; 4 g fat; 470 mg sodium.

TWO-DAY SHERRIED BLACK BEAN SOUP

8 ounces *dried black beans, soaked overnight in water to cover*
2 tablespoons *corn-oil margarine*
1 medium onion, *finely chopped (1 ½ cups)*
2 cloves garlic, *minced*
4 cups water
2 ribs celery, *without leaves, finely chopped (1 cup)*
¼ cup *finely chopped fresh parsley*
1 bay leaf
½ teaspoon salt
¼ teaspoon EACH *crushed dried thyme, crushed dried oregano, and freshly ground black pepper*
1 ham bone or ham hock
¼ cup *dry sherry*
½ cup *light sour cream, for garnish (optional)*
¼ cup *chopped fresh chives or scallion tops, for garnish (optional)*

1. Drain the beans, rinse thoroughly and set aside. Melt the margarine in a heavy pot over medium heat. Add the onion and garlic and cook until the onion is soft and translucent, about 10 minutes.

2. Add all remaining ingredients except the sherry, sour cream, and chopped chives. Bring to a boil, reduce the heat to low, and cook, covered, for 2 hours, stirring occasionally. Cool to room temperature and refrigerate uncovered all day or overnight.

3. Remove all of the congealed fat on the top of the soup. Remove the ham bone and the bay leaf. Spoon the soup into a food processor or a blender and process until smooth. Pour the soup back into the pot, add the sherry and reheat to the desired serving temperature.

4. To serve, spoon ¾ cup soup into each bowl and top with a dollop of sour cream and a sprinkling of chopped chives, if desired.

MAKES 6 CUPS, EIGHT ¾-CUP SERVINGS

Each serving contains approximately 215 calories; 5 mg cholesterol; 4 g fat; 316 mg sodium.

SIMPLE SPLIT PEA SOUP

1 pound dried split peas
8 cups water
1 ham or smoked pork hock
1 large onion, chopped (2 cups)
2 carrots, scraped and diced (1 cup)
2 ribs celery, without leaves, chopped (1 cup)
1 bay leaf
½ teaspoon salt
3 cups defatted chicken stock (see page 15)
Sherry (optional)

1. Place all the ingredients except the chicken stock and sherry in a large pot or soup kettle and bring to a boil over medium heat. Reduce the heat to low and simmer, covered, for 3 to 4 hours. Cool to room temperature and refrigerate overnight.

2. The next day, remove and discard the fat that has congealed on top. Remove the ham hock and separate the meat from the bone, discarding any remaining fat. Return the lean meat to the soup mixture.

3. In a blender or food processor, puree the soup, a little at a time, until smooth. Pour the pureed soup back into soup kettle, add the stock, and mix well. Bring the soup to a boil over medium heat, stirring constantly. Serve hot with a dash of sherry, if desired.

MAKES 11 CUPS, ELEVEN 1-CUP SERVINGS

Each serving contains approximately 190 calories; 10 mg cholesterol; 2 g fat; 155 mg sodium.

SALADS

※

FRESH FRUIT YOGURT AND PASTA SALAD

※

FOR THE TOPPING

4 cups sliced strawberries
¼ cup sugar
1 tablespoon fresh lemon juice

FOR THE SALAD

6 cups diced fresh fruit (your favorite kinds)
2 cups cooked orzo
1 cup plain nonfat yogurt

1. Combine all the topping ingredients in a saucepan and allow to stand for 10 minutes. Place over low heat and cook, stirring fre-

quently, until the juices start to boil. Allow to boil for 2 minutes, then remove from the heat and allow to cool to room temperature.

2. Combine all the salad ingredients and mix well. To serve, place about 2 cups of the salad onto each of four plates and spoon ¾ cup of the sauce over the top of each serving.

MAKES 4 SERVINGS

Each serving contains approximately 569 calories; 13 mg cholesterol; 2 g fat; 61 mg sodium.

TAILGATE PASTA SALAD

¼ cup fresh lime juice
2 tablespoons extra virgin olive oil
1 tablespoon sherry wine vinegar
½ teaspoon salt
½ teaspoon freshly ground black pepper
⅛ teaspoon red pepper flakes
½ pound orzo, cooked al dente
1 pound Roma tomatoes, peeled and diced
1 small red onion, diced (1 cup)
1 cup chopped cilantro (fresh coriander)
One 7 ½-ounce can lump crabmeat, flaked

1. Combine the lime juice, oil, vinegar, salt, pepper, and red pepper flakes. Mix well and pour over the cooked pasta. Allow to marinate for at least 1 hour.

2. Add the remaining ingredients to the marinated pasta and toss to mix well.

MAKES 6 CUPS, SIX 1-CUP SERVINGS

Each serving contains approximately 250 calories; 32 mg cholesterol; 6 g fat; 325 mg sodium.

SUMMER SEAFOOD PESTO SALAD

Two 6 ½-ounce cans chopped clams
½ cup packed fresh basil leaves
3 cloves garlic, peeled
¼ cup freshly grated Parmesan cheese
¼ teaspoon freshly ground black pepper
1 tablespoon extra virgin olive oil
12 ounces farfalle (bow-ties), cooked al dente (6 cups)

1. Drain the juice from the clams into a blender container or food processor. Set the clams aside. Add the basil, garlic, cheese, and pepper and blend or process until smooth. Leaving the machine running, slowly add the oil until it is completely incorporated.

2. Place the cooked pasta and the reserved clams in a large mixing bowl. Add the basil mixture and mix well. Serve at room temperature or refrigerate and serve cold.

MAKES 6 CUPS, FOUR 1 ½-CUP SERVINGS

Each serving contains approximately 487 calories; 61 mg cholesterol; 8 g fat; 187 mg sodium.

COLD CAPELLINI WITH SQUID

This recipe was created by David Hough, the Terrace Restaurant Chef at the Phoenician resort in Scotsdale, Arizona. He makes his own tomato vinegar for this tasty cold pasta dish. If you can't find it, just use any good wine vinegar as a substitute.

4 ounces cooked squid, thinly sliced (1 cup)
¼ cup tomato vinegar
¼ cup fresh lemon juice

½ teaspoon salt
¼ teaspoon freshly ground black pepper
12 ounces capellini, cooked al dente (5 ⅓ cups)
½ cup diced tomato
½ cup diced red onion
½ cup cooked peas
½ cup thinly sliced shiitake mushrooms
¼ cup Pesto Sauce (see page 70)
4 crusty whole-grain rolls

1. In a medium-size bowl, combine the squid, vinegar, lemon juice, salt, and pepper and mix well.

2. In large bowl, combine the cooked capellini and ¼ cup EACH of the tomato, onion, peas, and mushrooms. Toss to mix well and then add 2 tablespoons of the pesto sauce, again tossing to mix well.

3. To serve, divide the capellini evenly among each of four bowls. Top with the seasoned squid and garnish with a sprinkle of each of the remaining tomato, onion, peas, and mushrooms. Paint the edge of each bowl with the remaining pesto sauce and serve with the whole-grain rolls.

MAKES 4 SERVINGS

Each serving contains approximately 252 calories; 70 mg cholesterol; 8 g fat; 431 mg sodium.

THAI CHICKEN SALAD

This is a variation of the salad I designed for the University of California, San Diego, Faculty Club. I am delighted to tell you that it is one of the biggest selling items on their menu.

FOR THE DRESSING

6 *white kale leaves*

½ *cup water*

6 *tablespoons unhomogenized (old-fashioned) peanut butter*

2 *tablespoons reduced-sodium soy sauce*

2 *tablespoons dark sesame oil*

1 ½ *tablespoons chopped peeled fresh ginger*

1 *tablespoon dry sherry*

3 *cloves garlic, chopped (1 tablespoon)*

1 *tablespoon chopped scallions*

2 *teaspoons sugar*

¼ *teaspoon red pepper flakes*

FOR THE SALAD

8 *ounces Chuka Soba noodles, cooked according to package instructions*

1 *tablespoon dark sesame oil*

3 *cups shredded carrot, blanched*

1 *large red bell pepper, seeded and cut into thin strips (1 cup)*

1 *large yellow bell pepper, seeded and cut into thin strips (1 cup)*

3 *medium scallions, cut on the diagonal (1 cup)*

2 *cups mung bean sprouts*

Six *4-ounce boneless, skinless chicken breast halves, brushed with sesame*
  oil, grilled, and cut into thin strips

1 *large cucumber, spiral cut, for garnish (optional)*

Trimmed scallions, for garnish (optional)

1. Combine all the dressing ingredients in a blender and process until smooth. You should have about 2 cups dressing. Set aside.

2. To make the salad, toss the cooked noodles with 1 teaspoon of the sesame oil and set aside. Place the remaining 2 teaspoons oil in a large skillet over medium-high heat and stir-fry the carrots, bell pepper strips, and scallions until crisp-tender, 4 to 5 minutes, then set aside.

3. To serve, place ⅔ cup of the noodles on each of six plates. Top each serving with ⅓ cup of the mung bean sprouts and arrange the grilled, sliced chicken over the top. Dress each salad with ⅓ cup dress-

ing, and divide the stir-fried vegetable mixture evenly among each serving. Garnish with spiral cut cucumber and trimmed scallions, if desired.

MAKES 6 SERVINGS

Each serving contains approximately 477 calories; 66 mg cholesterol; 17 g fat; 564 mg sodium.

CHINESE CHICKEN SALAD

This is a variation on a classic that first appeared in my column years ago. It is one of my favorite salads and it is also good made with turkey, water-packed tuna, or shrimp, or a combination, instead of the chicken.

¼ cup almonds, chopped
8 ounces Chuka Soba noodles, cooked according to package instructions
1 pound fresh mushrooms, sliced (4 cups)
¾ pound cooked chicken breast, julienne cut (3 cups)
1 cup chopped scallion tops
1 cup snow peas, strings removed, ends notched in a V shape, and blanched
1 cup fresh bean sprouts
1 cup water chestnuts, julienne cut
1 cup Mandarin Dressing and Marinade (see page 24)
¼ cup julienne-cut red and yellow bell peppers, for garnish
4 scallion flowers, for garnish (see note on page 56)

1. Toast the almonds in a preheated 350°F oven until golden brown, 8 to 10 minutes. Watch carefully, as they burn easily. Set aside.

2. Combine the cooked noodles, mushrooms, chicken, scallions, snow peas, bean sprouts, water chestnuts, and Mandarin dressing and toss thoroughly.

3. Spoon 3 cups of the salad mixture onto each of four chilled plates and top each with 1 tablespoon toasted almonds and 1 table-spoon red and yellow bell peppers. Plant a scallion flower on the top of each serving.

Note:

To make a scallion flower, cut the bulb end off the scallion just below the green top. Cut the root end off of the bulb and shred the bulb by slicing it through first in half, then in quarters, then in eighths and so on until it looks shredded. To open the scallion flower, drop it in ice water and allow it to "bloom" before using.

MAKES 12 CUPS, FOUR 3-CUP SERVINGS

Each serving contains approximately 470 calories; 70 mg cholesterol; 14 g fat; 282 mg sodium.

PANTRY PASTA NIÇOISE

FOR THE DRESSING

¼ *cup red wine vinegar*
2 tablespoons Dijon mustard
1 clove garlic, pressed or minced
One 6-ounce jar marinated artichoke hearts, drained, liquid reserved

FOR THE SALAD

One 10-ounce package frozen French-cut green beans, thawed
8 ounces orzo, cooked al dente
One 6 ½-ounce can solid water-packed tuna, drained and flaked
2 Roma tomatoes, quartered
8 ripe olives
4 anchovy fillets, well drained (optional)
Chopped fresh parsley, for garnish (optional)

1. Combine the vinegar, mustard, garlic, and the reserved liquid from the artichokes and mix well. Set the drained artichoke hearts aside.

2. Pour the dressing over the thawed green beans and allow to marinate for at least 1 hour.

3. To serve, in a large bowl combine the reserved artichoke hearts with the cooked pasta, tossing to mix well. Pour the dressing and green beans in the bowl and again mix well. Divide the mixture among each of four plates. Arrange the flaked tuna on the top of each serving and garnish each salad with 2 tomato wedges and 2 olives. Place an anchovy and sprig of parsley on top, if desired.

MAKES 6 CUPS, FOUR 1 ½-CUP SERVINGS

Each serving contains approximately 548 calories; 56 mg cholesterol; 13 g fat; 2503 mg sodium.

JASMINE RICE SALAD

2 tablespoons rice vinegar
1 tablespoon fresh lime juice
1 tablespoon dark sesame oil
½ teaspoon salt
¼ teaspoon freshly ground black pepper
⅛ teaspoon red pepper flakes or to taste
3 cups cooked jasmine rice (or any long-grain white rice)
1 red bell pepper, seeded, and finely chopped
½ pound snow peas, blanched and thinly sliced
2 scallions, finely chopped
¼ cup loosely packed chopped cilantro (fresh coriander)

1. In a small bowl, combine the vinegar, lime juice, oil, salt, pepper, and red pepper flakes and stir until the salt is completely dissolved and the oil is completely incorporated.

2. In a large bowl, combine the remaining ingredients and toss to mix well. Pour the dressing over the rice mixture and again toss to mix well. Serve immediately or, if preparing ahead of time, refrigerate the dressing and salad separately, tightly covered, and combine them just before serving.

MAKES ABOUT 6 CUPS, SIX 1-CUP SERVINGS

Each serving contains approximtely 173 calories; no cholesterol; 3 g fat; 198 mg sodium.

BROWN RICE SALAD WITH SPINACH AND ALMONDS

¼ *cup chopped almonds*
2 ½ *cups defatted chicken stock (see page 15)*
¾ *cup long-grain brown rice*
2 *teaspoons olive oil*
1 *cup chopped scallions*
4 *ounces fresh spinach leaves, thoroughly washed and drained, stems and large veins removed, and chopped*
¼ *teaspoon salt (omit if using salted stock)*
¼ *teaspoon freshly ground black pepper*
1 *teaspoon fresh lemon juice*

1. Preheat the oven to 350°F. Place the almonds on an ungreased baking sheet or in a pie pan and bake until a golden brown, 8 to 10 minutes. Watch carefully, as they burn easily. Set aside.

2. Bring the chicken stock to a boil in a saucepan over medium-high heat. Stir in the rice, reduce the heat to low, and cook, covered, until the rice is tender, about 45 minutes. Set aside to cool.

3. While the rice is cooking, place the oil in a skillet over low heat. Add the scallions and stir-fry for 2 minutes. Add the scallions, spinach, salt, pepper, and lemon juice to the cooked rice and mix well.

Garnish each serving with 1 tablespoon of the toasted almonds. Serve at room temperature or refrigerate and serve cold.

MAKES ABOUT 2 CUPS, FOUR ½-CUP SERVINGS

Each serving contains approximately 237 calories; negligible cholesterol; 9 g fat; 477 mg sodium.

WILD RICE SALAD À L'ORANGE

¾ cup wild rice
2 cups defatted chicken stock (see page 15)
2 tablespoons grated orange zest
1 teaspoon dried thyme, crushed
½ cup chopped almonds
1 tablespoon extra virgin olive oil

1. In a medium-size saucepan over medium heat, combine the rice, stock, orange zest, and thyme. Bring to a boil, reduce the heat to low, and simmer, covered, until all liquid is absorbed and the rice is fluffy, 55 to 65 minutes. Remove from the heat and set aside to cool.

2. Preheat the oven to 350°F. Place the almonds on an ungreased baking sheet or in a pie pan and bake until a golden brown, 8 to 10 minutes. Watch carefully, as they burn easily.

3. Combine the cooled, cooked rice, the almonds, and oil and mix thoroughly. Serve at room temperature or refrigerate, tightly covered, and serve cold.

MAKES EIGHT ½-CUP SERVINGS

Each serving contains approximately 135 calories; no cholesterol; 7 g fat; 122 mg sodium.

PEANUT APPLE SLAW

FOR THE DRESSING

⅓ cup crunchy unhomogenized (old-fashioned) peanut butter
⅔ cup nonfat sour cream substitute
3 tablespoons cider vinegar
3 tablespoons fresh orange juice
1 tablespoon sugar
¼ teaspoon salt

FOR THE SALAD

3 cups shredded cabbage
2 cups diced red Delicious apples
¼ cup raisins
8 cabbage leaves (optional)

1. Combine all the dressing ingredients and blend until smooth.

2. Combine all the salad ingredients, except the cabbage leaves, in a large bowl. Pour in the dressing and toss to mix well. Serve in cabbage leaves, if desired.

MAKES ABOUT 6 CUPS, EIGHT ¾-CUP SERVINGS

Each serving contains approximately 134 calories; no cholesterol; 6 g fat; 95 mg sodium.

TOMATO, CORN, AND BLACK BEAN SALAD

3 Roma tomatoes, peeled and diced
½ teaspoon salt
1 medium onion, finely chopped (1 ½ cups)
¼ teaspoon freshly ground black pepper
¼ teaspoon ground cumin
⅛ teaspoon dried oregano, crushed
⅛ teaspoon ground cayenne pepper
1 cup fresh or frozen corn kernels, thawed
One 16-ounce can black beans, drained
1 tablespoon extra virgin olive oil

1. Place the tomatoes in a colander, sprinkle with the salt, and toss to mix well. Allow to drain for 1 hour.

2. Put the onion in a heavy saucepan and cook, covered, over low heat until soft and translucent, about 10 to 15 minutes. Stir occasionally and add a little water or stock, if necessary, to prevent scorching.

3. Add all remaining ingredients except the tomatoes and oil and cook, uncovered, for 5 minutes, stirring frequently. Remove from the heat and allow to cool. Add the drained tomatoes and olive oil and mix well.

MAKES ABOUT 3 CUPS, SIX ½-CUP SERVINGS

Each serving contains approximately 179 calories; no cholesterol; 3 g fat; 381 mg sodium.

FAVA BEAN SALAD

½ cup reduced-fat mayonnaise
2 tablespoons brown mustard
1 teaspoon prepared horseradish
¼ teaspoon salt
One 8-ounce can water chestnuts, drained and chopped
1 small red onion, chopped (1 cup)
1 cup diced celery
2 cups cooked fava beans
Radicchio leaves (optional)

Combine the mayonnaise, mustard, horseradish, and salt and mix well. Add all remaining ingredients and again mix well. Serve on radicchio leaves, if desired.

MAKES ABOUT 5 CUPS, FOUR 1 ¼-CUP SERVINGS

Each serving contains approximately 211 calories; 7 mg cholesterol; 7 g fat; 850 mg sodium.

LEBANESE LENTIL SALAD

FOR THE LENTILS

2 large onions, finely chopped (3 cups)
4 cloves garlic, minced or pressed
¾ teaspoon salt
¾ teaspoon ground cinnamon
¾ teaspoon ground allspice
2 cups dried lentils, rinsed and drained
½ cup long-grain brown rice, rinsed and drained
5 cups water

FOR THE SALAD

1 head Romaine lettuce, torn into bite-size pieces
1 green bell pepper, seeded and thinly sliced
1 small cucumber, peeled, seeded, and diced
1 tablespoon fresh lemon juice
¼ teaspoon salt
3 tablespoons rice vinegar
2 cloves garlic, pressed or minced
2 tablespoons extra virgin olive oil
½ cup crumbled feta cheese (2 ounces)
8 Roma tomatoes, quartered, for garnish

1. To make the lentils, combine the chopped onions, garlic, salt, cinnamon, and allspice in a 2-quart saucepan and cook, covered, over low heat, until the onion is soft and translucent, about 10 to 15 minutes. Stir occasionally and add a little water or stock, if necessary, to prevent scorching.

2. Increase the heat to medium and add the drained lentils and rice and continue to cook, stirring, for 5 more minutes. Add the water and bring to a boil. Cover, and cook over low heat until the liquid is absorbed and the rice is tender, about 1 hour. Makes about 7 cups.

3. While the lentil mixture is cooking, make the salad and dressing. In a large bowl, combine the lettuce, bell pepper, and cucumber and mix well. In a small bowl, combine the lemon juice and salt and stir until the salt is completely dissolved. Add the vinegar and garlic and mix well. Slowly beat in the oil until well combined. Pour the dressing mixture over the salad mixture. Add the cheese and toss thoroughly. You should have about 8 cups.

4. To serve, divide the lentil mixture evenly among eight plates, a generous ¾-cup each. Top with about 1 cup of the salad mixture and garnish each serving with 4 tomato quarters.

MAKES 8 SERVINGS

Each serving contains approximately 322 calories; 6 mg cholesterol; 6 g fat; 389 mg sodium.

GREEK SALAD WITH SPROUTED BEANS

6 tablespoons fresh lemon juice
2 tablespoons extra virgin olive oil
Freshly ground black pepper, to taste
¾ cup mixed sprouted canned beans (lentil, adzuki, garbanzo, etc.)
6 cups bite-size pieces assorted young lettuce leaves
6 Roma tomatoes, quartered
1 green bell pepper, seeded and cut into strips
18 Greek olives
1 red onion, cut into rings
3 ounces feta cheese, crumbled

1. In a small bowl, mix the lemon juice, oil, and black pepper. Pour over the sprouted beans and set aside.

2. Arrange 1 cup of the lettuce on each of six plates. Add 4 tomato quarters, slices of bell pepper, 3 olives, onion rings, and ½ ounce of the cheese to each salad. Top each serving with 2 tablespoons of the marinated sprouts and a little of the marinade.

MAKES 6 SERVINGS

Each serving contains approximately 173 calories; 13 mg cholesterol; 11 g fat; 789 mg sodium.

LENTIL AND RAISIN SALAD

¼ cup chopped black walnuts
¼ cup raisins
½ cup diced pineapple, canned in juice
2 tablespoons plain nonfat yogurt
1 tablespoon reduced-calorie mayonnaise
2 cups cooked lentils
Lettuce leaves, for garnish
Fresh mint sprigs, for garnish

1. Preheat the oven to 350°F. Toast the walnuts in the preheated oven until a golden brown, 8 to 10 minutes. Watch carefully, they burn easily. Set aside.

2. Soak the raisins in warm water until plump, about 20 minutes.

3. Drain the pineapple, reserving 3 tablespoons of the juice. Set aside.

4. In a medium-size bowl, combine the yogurt, mayonnaise, and pineapple juice and mix well. Add the lentils and pineapple and again mix well. Drain the raisins, add to the lentil mixture, and again mix well. Chill thoroughly.

5. Just before serving, add the walnuts to the lentil mixture and mix well. To serve, line six chilled salad plates with lettuce leaves. Top with ½ cup of the lentil mixture and garnish with mint sprigs.

MAKES ABOUT 3 CUPS, SIX ½-CUP SERVINGS

Each serving contains approximately 155 calories; 1 mg cholesterol; 4 g fat; 174 mg sodium.

BLACK-EYED PEA AND SHRIMP SALAD

½ pound black-eyed peas, soaked overnight in water to cover, rinsed, and drained

1 bay leaf

1 teaspoon coriander seeds

1 teaspoon red pepper flakes

1 teaspoon cumin seeds

2 cinnamon sticks, broken

¼ teaspoon fresh lime juice

¾ teaspoon salt

1 tablespoon sherry vinegar

1 tablespoon extra virgin olive oil

1 teaspoon freshly ground black pepper

½ pound cooked shrimp

½ cup packed coarsely chopped cilantro (fresh coriander)

1. Place the drained black-eyed peas in a pan. Add the bay leaf, coriander, red pepper flakes, cumin seed, and cinnamon sticks. Add cold water to cover by 2 inches and bring to a boil over medium-high heat. Reduce the heat to low and simmer, covered, until the peas are tender, about 45 minutes.

2. Combine the lime juice and salt and stir until the salt is dissolved. Add the vinegar, oil, and pepper and mix well. Add the shrimp and again mix well. Add the black-eyed peas and cilantro and toss thoroughly. Serve at room temperature.

MAKES 4 SERVINGS

Each serving contains approximately 137 calories; 111 mg cholesterol; 4 g fat; 706 mg sodium.

GARBANZO BEAN AND ALBACORE SALAD

Two 16-ounce cans garbanzo beans, rinsed and drained
¼ cup chopped fresh basil
¼ cup packed chopped fresh parsley
¼ cup finely chopped red onion
2 tablespoons extra virgin olive oil
2 cloves garlic, pressed or minced
¼ teaspoon salt
¼ teaspoon freshly ground black pepper
One 12 ½-ounce can water-packed albacore tuna, drained and broken into chunks
Radicchio leaves, for garnish (optional)

1. Combine the drained beans with the basil, parsley, and onion and mix well.

2. Warm the oil in a skillet over medium heat and cook the garlic just until it starts to sizzle. Remove from the heat, add the salt and pepper, and mix well. Add the tuna and toss thoroughly. Serve on radicchio leaves, if desired.

MAKES ABOUT 4 ½ CUPS, SIX ¾-CUP SERVINGS

Each serving contains approximately 565 calories; 36 mg cholesterol; 15 g fat; 1038 mg sodium.

VEGETABLE SIDE DISHES AND VEGETARIAN ENTRÉES

LEMON COUSCOUS

This couscous is a particularly good side dish with fish or poultry. However, I also like it with the Lamb Fricassee with Field Vegetables and Garbanzo Beans on page 221.

2 cups defatted chicken stock (see page 15)
¼ teaspoon salt (omit if using salted stock)
¼ teaspoon freshly ground black pepper
1 cinnamon stick, broken in half
2 tablespoons fresh lemon juice
1 teaspoon fresh lemon zest
2 teaspoons extra virgin olive oil
1 cup (6 ⅔ ounces) couscous

1. Combine the stock, salt, pepper, cinnamon stick, lemon juice and zest, and oil in a saucepan with a tight-fitting lid. Bring to a boil and remove from the heat.

2. Stir in the couscous, cover tightly, and allow to stand for 5 minutes. Uncover, remove the cinnamon stick, and fluff the couscous with a fork.

MAKES 3 CUPS, SIX ½-CUP SERVINGS

Each serving contains approximately 36 calories; 0 mg cholesterol; 2 g fat; 258 mg sodium.

SPAGHETTI WITH MARINARA SAUCE

1 medium onion, chopped (1 ½ cups)
1 medium green bell pepper, seeded and chopped (1 cup)
1 rib celery, without leaves, chopped (½ cup)
1 shallot, chopped
2 cloves garlic, pressed or minced
One 28-ounce can crushed tomatoes
One 15-ounce can tomato sauce
1 tablespoon tightly packed minced fresh parsley
1 teaspoon dried oregano, crushed
1 teaspoon dried basil, crushed
¼ teaspoon dried thyme, crushed
¼ teaspoon minced fresh or dried rosemary
½ teaspoon sugar
½ teaspoon salt
¼ teaspoon freshly ground black pepper
¼ teaspoon red pepper flakes
½ teaspoon balsamic vinegar
1 ½ pounds spaghetti, cooked al dente
1 tablespoon extra virgin olive oil

1. In a large heavy saucepan over low heat, cook the onion, pepper, celery, shallot, and garlic, covered, until soft, 10 to 15 minutes.

Stir occasionally and add a little water or stock, if necessary, to prevent scorching.

2. Add the remaining ingredients except the vinegar, spaghetti, and olive oil. Bring to a boil over medium heat, then reduce the heat to low and cook, covered, for at least one hour. Remove from the heat, add the vinegar, and mix well.

3. Thoroughly drain the cooked pasta and toss with the olive oil. To serve, place 1 ½ cups pasta on each of six plates. Top each serving with ¾ cup of the marinara sauce.

MAKES 6 SERVINGS

Each serving contains approximately 310 calories; no cholesterol; 3 g fat; 645 mg sodium.

LINGUINI WITH PESTO SAUCE

¼ *cup pine nuts*
2 *cups tightly packed fresh basil leaves*
2 *cups tightly packed fresh spinach leaves, stems and veins removed*
4 *cloves garlic, finely chopped*
4 *ounces imported Parmesan cheese, freshly grated (1 cup)*
½ *teaspoon fresh lemon juice*
¼ *teaspoon salt*
¼ *teaspoon freshly ground black pepper*
½ *cup extra virgin olive oil*
2 *pounds linguini, cooked al dente*

1. On an ungreased baking sheet or in a pie pan, toast the pine nuts in a preheated 350°F oven until a golden brown, 8 to 10 minutes. Watch carefully, as they burn easily.

2. Combine all ingredients except the linguini in a blender or food processor fitted with the metal blade. Process on high until a smooth paste is formed.

3. To serve, combine the pesto sauce with the cooked linguini and toss to mix well, or serve 1 ¼ cups linguini on each of eight plates and top with ¼ cup of the pesto sauce.

MAKES 8 SERVINGS

Each serving contains approximately 370 calories; 49 mg cholesterol; 21 g fat; 359 mg sodium.

VEGETARIAN DELIGHT

3 *cups cooked pasta (about 8 ounces dry pasta, depending upon the type)*
2 *cups hot Marinara Sauce (see page 24)*
4 *cups hot steamed fresh vegetables, a colorful assortment of your favorite kinds*
2 *ounces imported Parmesan cheese, freshly grated (½ cup)*
¼ *cup packed chopped fresh basil leaves*

1. Place ¾ cup pasta on each of four warm plates. Top each serving with ½ cup of the marinara sauce.

2. Place 1 cup of the hot vegetables on top of each serving and sprinkle 2 tablespoons cheese over the top of the vegetables. Garnish each serving with 1 tablespoon fresh basil.

MAKES 4 SERVINGS

Each serving contains approximately 145 calories; no cholesterol; 3 g fat; 310 mg sodium.

CREAMY SPINACH PASTA WITH SUN-DRIED TOMATOES

This recipe is also a wonderful base for pasta primavera. Add steamed fresh vegetables of your choice—or use leftovers!

½ cup sun-dried tomatoes (½ ounce)
One 12-ounce can evaporated skimmed milk (1 ½ cups)
1 ½ cups low-fat cottage cheese
2 cloves garlic, quartered
½ teaspoon salt
½ teaspoon freshly ground black pepper
⅛ teaspoon red pepper flakes
3 ounces Parmesan cheese, freshly grated (¾ cup)
2 tablespoons extra virgin olive oil
1 pound spinach fettuccine noodles, cooked al dente
¾ cup packed chopped fresh basil leaves

1. Using scissors, cut the sun-dried tomatoes into pieces. Put them in a bowl and cover with hot water. Allow to stand for 10 minutes. Drain well and set aside.

2. In a blender container, combine the milk, cottage cheese, garlic, salt, pepper, red pepper flakes, and Parmesan cheese. Process until smooth. Leave the blender running and slowly add the oil until well blended. Pour the sauce into a heavy saucepan and warm over low heat; do not boil.

3. Drain the cooked, hot fettuccine and put in a bowl. Pour the sauce over the noodles, add the drained sun-dried tomatoes and the basil and toss to mix well.

MAKES 8 CUPS; SIX 1 ⅓-CUP SERVINGS

Each serving contains approximately 314 calories; 43 mg cholesterol; 11 g fat; 766 mg sodium.

LIGHT LINGUINE

1 tablespoon corn-oil margarine
1 medium onion, finely chopped (1 ½ cups)
2 cloves garlic, pressed or minced
⅛ teaspoon ground nutmeg
⅛ teaspoon freshly ground black pepper
¾ cup loosely packed finely chopped fresh parsley
½ cup loosely packed finely chopped fresh basil
1 tablespoon cornstarch
¾ cup nonfat milk
½ cup defatted chicken stock (see page 15)
1 ounce Parmesan cheese, freshly grated (¼ cup)
12 ounces linguine noodles, cooked al dente (4 cups)

1. Melt the margarine in a large skillet over low heat. Add the onion, garlic, nutmeg, pepper, parsley, and basil and cook, stirring frequently, until the onion is soft and translucent, 10 to 15 minutes.

2. In a saucepan, combine the cornstarch and the milk and stir until the cornstarch is completely dissolved. Add the chicken stock and cheese and bring to a simmer over low heat. Cook, stirring constantly, until thickened.

3. Add the cornstarch mixture to the onion mixture and mix well. Pour over the cooked linguine and toss to blend evenly.

MAKES ABOUT 4 CUPS, FOUR 1-CUP SERVINGS

Each serving contains approximately 231 calories; 34 mg cholesterol; 6 g fat; 264 mg sodium.

MACARONI AND CHEDDAR CHEESE

1 tablespoon corn-oil margarine
3 tablespoons unbleached all-purpose flour
2 ½ cups nonfat milk, at a simmer
¼ teaspoon salt
¼ teaspoon freshly ground black pepper
⅛ teaspoon ground nutmeg
3 to 4 drops Tabasco sauce
8 ounces reduced-fat sharp Cheddar cheese, shredded (2 cups)
8 ounces elbow macaroni, cooked al dente (4 cups)
¾ cup fresh whole-wheat bread crumbs

1. Preheat the oven to 350°F. Melt the margarine in a heavy saucepan over low heat. Add the flour and cook, stirring, for 2 minutes; do not brown.

2. Remove the pan from the heat and add the simmering milk, stirring constantly with a wire whisk. Add the salt, pepper, and nutmeg. Return the pan to the heat and simmer, slowly, until thickened, 15 to 20 minutes, stirring occasionally.

3. Remove the pan from the heat and add the Tabasco sauce and cheese. Mix well and set the sauce aside.

4. Spray a 2-quart casserole with a nonstick vegetable coating. Add the cooked macaroni and the cheese sauce and mix well. Top with the bread crumbs and spray them lightly with the vegetable coating. Bake in the preheated oven until bubbly and lightly browned on the top, 20 to 30 minutes.

MAKES ABOUT 5 CUPS, FOUR 1 ¼ CUP SERVINGS

Each serving contains approximately 369 calories; 31 mg cholesterol; 14 g fat; 577 mg sodium.

SPAGHETTI-PARMESAN SOUFFLÉ

¼ pound spaghetti, broken into 2-inch pieces
1 tablespoon extra virgin olive oil
1 clove garlic, minced
1 large egg yolk
2 cups light sour cream
1 cup freshly grated Parmesan cheese
¼ cup packed finely chopped fresh parsley
½ teaspoon salt
¼ teaspoon freshly ground black pepper
3 large egg whites

1. Preheat the oven to 350°F. Spray a 6-cup soufflé dish or oven-proof casserole with nonstick vegetable coating and set aside. Cook the spaghetti al dente and drain well.

2. Place the oil in a large skillet over medium heat. Add the garlic and cook just until it starts to sizzle. Add the drained spaghetti and stir-fry until well mixed. Set aside.

3. In a large mixing bowl, combine the egg yolk and sour cream and mix well. Add the cheese, parsley, salt, pepper, and spaghetti and mix well.

4. In a separate mixing bowl, beat the egg whites until stiff but not dry. Fold the whites into spaghetti mixture just until no streaks of white show. Spoon the mixture into the prepared dish or casserole and set the dish in another, larger dish or pan that is at least 3 inches deep. Add hot water to the larger pan to a depth of 2 inches and bake in the preheated oven until lightly browned and puffy, about 45 minutes.

MAKES ABOUT 6 CUPS, SIX 1-CUP SERVINGS

Each serving contains approximately 282 calories; 58 mg cholesterol; 13 g fat; 571 mg sodium.

FUSILLI WITH EGGPLANT AND MOZZARELLA

If you have young tender eggplant you may not need to peel it. Salting and draining the eggplant first enables you to cook the eggplant with less oil. If you are concerned about the salt then rinse the eggplant well before patting it dry or eliminate the salt altogether by blanching the eggplant before adding it to the onion mixture.

1 pound eggplant, peeled and diced
1 teaspoon salt
1 medium onion, finely chopped (1 ½ cups)
4 cloves garlic, pressed or minced
1 tablespoon olive oil
1 ½ pounds Roma tomatoes, diced
¼ teaspoon freshly ground black pepper
1 pound fusilli, cooked al dente
½ cup shredded fresh basil leaves
½ pound part skim mozzarella cheese, shredded (2 cups)

1. Toss the diced eggplant and salt in a colander and allow to drain for 30 minutes.

2. Combine the onion and garlic in a heavy pan and cook, covered, over low heat until soft, about 10 to 15 minutes. Stir occasionally and add a little water or stock, if necessary, to prevent scorching.

3. Lightly press the excess moisture from the drained eggplant and pat dry with paper towels. Add the eggplant and oil to the onion mixture and cook, stirring frequently, over medium-low heat until the eggplant is tender, about 8 minutes.

4. Add the tomatoes and pepper and cook, covered, for 10 minutes. Add the cooked pasta, basil, and mozzarella and toss thoroughly. Serve immediately.

MAKES ABOUT 10 CUPS, SIX 1 ⅔-CUP SERVINGS

Each serving contains approximately 306 calories; 55 mg cholesterol; 5 g fat; 426 mg sodium.

ZUCCHINI MANICOTTI

14 manicotti shells
1 large onion, finely chopped (2 cups)
1 clove garlic, pressed or minced
1 pound zucchini (2 medium), shredded (3 cups)
One 15-ounce carton low-fat ricotta cheese
4 ounces reduced-fat sharp Cheddar cheese, shredded (1 cup)
½ teaspoon salt
¼ teaspoon freshly ground black pepper
1 teaspoon dried basil, crushed
½ teaspoon dried oregano, crushed
One 15-ounce can tomato sauce
4 ounces Parmesan cheese, shredded (1 cup)

1. Cook the manicotti shells according to the package instructions until tender. Be careful not to overcook them or they will tear. Drain and rinse in cold water, then place on waxed paper or a nonstick surface and set aside.

2. In a large nonstick skillet, combine the onion, garlic, and zucchini and cook, covered, over low heat until the onion is soft and translucent, 10 to 15 minutes. Stir occasionally and add a little water or stock if necessary to prevent scorching.

3. Remove the mixture from the heat and add the ricotta and Cheddar cheeses, the salt, pepper, basil, and oregano. Mix well and then stuff the mixture into the manicotti shells using your fingers, a

pastry tube, or a small spoon. Be careful not to tear the shells. Reserve the leftover filling for the sauce.

4. Preheat the oven to 350°F. Arrange the stuffed shells in a 9-by 13-inch glass baking dish which has been sprayed with nonstick vegetable coating. Combine the leftover filling with the tomato sauce and spoon the sauce over the stuffed shells. Cover and bake for 30 minutes. Uncover, top with the Parmesan cheese and return to the oven until hot and bubbly, about 10 minutes longer.

MAKES SEVEN 2-MANICOTTI SERVINGS

Each serving contains approximately 410 calories; 39 mg cholesterol; 13 g fat; 984 mg sodium.

PUMPKIN PAPPARDELLE

1 tablespoon olive oil
4 leeks, white part only, thinly sliced (4 cups)
½ teaspoon dried oregano, crushed
½ teaspoon dried basil, crushed
½ teaspoon dried thyme, crushed
1 teaspoon salt
¼ teaspoon freshly ground black pepper
⅛ teaspoon red pepper flakes
One 12-ounce can evaporated skimmed milk (1 ½ cups)
One 16-ounce can pumpkin
2 ounces Parmesan cheese, freshly grated (½ cup)
1 pound pappardelle, cooked al dente (6 cups)

1. Heat the oil in a 2-quart saucepan. Add the leeks and cook, covered, over low heat until soft, about 10 minutes. Add the oregano, basil, thyme, salt, pepper, and pepper flakes and mix well. Add 1 cup of the milk and cook, uncovered, over medium heat until reduced in volume by one fourth.

2. Put the remaining ½ cup milk and the pumpkin in a blender and blend until smooth. Pour the pumpkin mixture into the saucepan with the leek mixture and mix well. Bring to a simmer and add the Parmesan cheese. Cook, stirring constantly, until the cheese is melted. Makes about 4 cups sauce.

3. To serve, place 1 cup of the cooked pasta on each of six warm plates and top with ⅔ cup of the pumpkin sauce.

MAKES 6 SERVINGS

Each serving contains approximately 408 calories; 65 mg cholesterol; 7 g fat; 673 mg sodium.

WHOLE-WHEAT SPINACH LASAGNA

1 small onion, thinly sliced
6 ounces fresh mushrooms, sliced
8 ounces whole-wheat lasagna noodles, cooked al dente
1 tablespoon olive oil
2 pounds fresh spinach leaves, stems and veins removed, thoroughly washed, and drained
2 cloves garlic, pressed or minced
1 teaspoon dried basil, crushed
½ teaspoon dried oregano, crushed
¼ teaspoon freshly ground black pepper
1 ½ cups low-fat ricotta cheese
1 ounce Parmesan cheese, freshly grated (¼ cup)
1 large egg plus 1 egg white, lightly beaten
2 tablespoons chopped fresh parsley
Pinch of ground nutmeg
Freshly ground black pepper
Three 8-ounce cans prepared tomato sauce
3 ounces low-fat mozzarella cheese, grated (¾ cup)

1. Combine the onion and mushrooms in a medium-size saucepan and cook, covered, over low heat until the onions are soft and translucent, 10 to 15 minutes. Stir occasionally and add a little water or stock, if necessary, to prevent scorching.

2. While the onions are cooking, brush the lasagna noodles with the oil and set aside. Steam the spinach over rapidly boiling water until just wilted, 1 to 2 minutes. Press and squeeze to remove the excess water. Chop the spinach and add it to the onion mixture along with the garlic, basil, oregano, and pepper, and cook for 5 minutes.

4. In a medium-size bowl, combine the ricotta and Parmesan cheeses, the egg and egg white, and parsley. Season with the nutmeg and pepper to taste.

5. Preheat the oven to 400°F. Spray a 9- by 13-inch glass baking dish with olive oil–flavored nonstick vegetable coating and spread 1 cup of the tomato sauce in the bottom. Layer with a third of the lasagna noodles, half of the ricotta cheese mixture, and half of the spinach mixture. Layer with another third of the noodles, the remaining ricotta cheese mixture, and the remaining spinach mixture. Top with the remaining noodles and tomato sauce. Sprinkle the grated mozzarella cheese evenly over the top and bake until hot and bubbly, about 20 minutes.

MAKES 8 SERVINGS

Each serving contains approximately 310 calories; 50 mg cholesterol; 10 g fat; 805 mg sodium.

PENNE WITH WILD MUSHROOMS, BELL PEPPERS, AND ROASTED GARLIC

This is my favorite recipe from Bice restaurant in San Diego. I asked the executive chef, Patrick Clark, if he would allow me to share the recipe with my readers and, thankfully, he obliged.

6 heads garlic, peeled (about 50 cloves)
2 cups nonfat milk
6 tablespoons olive oil
½ pound wild mushrooms (morels, shiitake, etc.), stems removed and
    sliced (2 cups)
2 shallots, finely chopped
1 jalapeño pepper, seeded and finely chopped
2 cups defatted chicken stock (see page 15)
½ teaspoon salt (omit if using salted stock)
¼ teaspoon freshly ground black pepper
1 pound penne, cooked al dente
1 red bell pepper, roasted, seeded, peeled and diced
1 yellow bell pepper, roasted, seeded, peeled and diced
½ cup chopped fresh parsley

1. Combine the garlic cloves and milk in a saucepan and bring to a boil. Reduce the heat to low and cook, covered, for 5 minutes. Drain well. (Save the milk to make soup or garlic custard.) Place the drained garlic in a baking dish and toss with 2 tablespoons of the oil. Bake at 275°F until soft, about 45 minutes. Puree the roasted garlic and set aside.

2. Heat 2 more teaspoons of the oil in a medium skillet and cook the sliced mushrooms and 1 of the shallots over medium heat until soft, about 10 minutes, stirring occasionally. Remove to a bowl and set aside.

3. In the same pan, heat the remaining 2 teaspoons oil and cook the remaining shallot and the jalapeño until soft. Add the stock and bring to a boil over medium heat. Stir in the salt, pepper, mushrooms, pureed garlic, and pasta. Bring back to a boil, then remove from the heat and toss in the roasted peppers and chopped parsley. Serve immediately.

MAKES 12 CUPS, SIX 2-CUP SERVINGS

Each serving contains approximately 425 calories; negligible cholesterol; 7 g
fat; 325 mg sodium.

VEGETARIAN PASTITSIO

This dish is good hot, cold, or at room temperature. Tempeh is a textured vegetable protein found in health food stores. It is available seasoned and unseasoned and is usually kept in the frozen food section of the store. You can also substitute cooked rice or lentils for the tempeh, if you wish.

FOR THE TEMPEH MIXTURE

2 small onions, chopped (2 cups)
1 pound unseasoned tempeh
One 14 ½-ounce can ready-cut tomatoes, drained
One 8-ounce can tomato sauce
½ teaspoon salt
½ teaspoon dried oregano, crushed
¼ teaspoon ground cinnamon
⅛ teaspoon freshly ground black pepper

FOR THE WHITE SAUCE

3 tablespoons corn-oil margarine
⅓ cup whole-wheat flour
2 ½ cups nonfat milk, at a simmer
½ teaspoon salt
¼ teaspoon ground cinnamon
⅛ teaspoon ground white pepper
3 large egg whites, lightly beaten
½ cup low-fat ricotta cheese
12 ounces elbow macaroni or tube pasta, cooked al dentes
4 ounces Romano cheese, freshly grated (1 cup)

1. In large covered saucepan over low heat, cook the onions until soft and translucent, about 10 to 15 minutes. Stir occasionally and add a little water, if necessary, to prevent scorching. Add the tempeh and cook until no longer pink, about 5 minutes. Add the tomatoes, toma-

to sauce, and seasonings. Mix well, cover, and simmer over low heat for 40 minutes, stirring occasionally.

2. While the mixture is cooking, make the white sauce. Melt the margarine in a skillet over medium heat. Add the flour and cook 3 minutes, stirring constantly; be careful not to brown the flour. Add the simmering milk and stir constantly until smooth. Add the salt, cinnamon, and pepper and cook, stirring frequently, until thickened. Remove from the heat and slowly add the egg whites, stirring constantly. Combine 1 cup of sauce with the ricotta cheese, mix well, and set aside.

3. Preheat the oven to 350°F. Spray a 9- by 13-inch glass baking dish with nonstick vegetable coating. Spread half the cooked macaroni in the dish and top with the tempeh mixture. Pour the white sauce without the cheese evenly over the top. Sprinkle half the grated Romano cheese over the top and cover with the remaining macaroni. Bake for 30 minutes.

4. Remove the dish from the oven and increase the oven temperature to 400°F. Spread the reserved cheese and white sauce mixture over the top and sprinkle evenly with the remaining Romano cheese. Bake until slightly browned, another 20 to 30 minutes. Cool 10 minutes before serving.

MAKES NINE 1 ⅓-CUP SERVINGS

Each serving contains approximately 380 calories; 19 mg cholesterol; 13 g fat; 624 mg sodium.

VEGETARIAN POTSTICKERS

Chinese chili sauce is available in the ethnic foods section of many markets and in all oriental markets. Wonton skins are packaged, ready to use, and are often in the same section of your supermarket as the cheeses.

1 *pound fresh spinach leaves, thoroughly washed, stems and large veins*
   removed, and chopped
2 *large egg whites, lightly beaten*
1 *tablespoon reduced-sodium soy sauce*
1 *teaspoon Chinese chili sauce*
1 ½ *tablespoons minced peeled fresh ginger*
3 *scallions, minced*
1 ½ *cups cooked brown rice*
½ *cup water*
1 *teaspoon reduced-sodium Worcestershire sauce*
½ *teaspoon sugar*
2 *teaspoons grated lemon zest, yellow part only*
32 *wonton skins*
Cornstarch
2 *tablespoons peanut oil*

1. Blanch the spinach in boiling water for about 15 seconds. Drain thoroughly, being careful to squeeze out all moisture.

2. In a large bowl, combine the egg whites, soy sauce, ½ teaspoon of the chili sauce, the ginger, and scallions, and mix thoroughly. Add the blanched spinach and the rice and mix thoroughly again.

3. In a separate bowl, combine the water, Worcestershire sauce, the remaining chili sauce, the sugar, and lemon rind; set aside.

4. Separate the wonton skins and place 1 tablespoon of the rice mixture onto each of the wonton skins. To form into potstickers, bring the 4 corners of each wonton skin into the center, overlapping to cover the filling and form a ball. Place the ball, fold side down, in the soft hollow of your hand between your thumb and index finger. Squeeze your hand together, gently, to form and seal each potsticker.

5. Place the finished potstickers on a large baking sheet which has been lightly dusted with cornstarch and refrigerate, uncovered. The recipe can be assembled to this point several hours ahead of time and should be done at least one hour in advance.

6. To cook the potstickers, heat the peanut oil in a large nonstick skillet over medium-high heat. Add the potstickers and cook until the

bottoms are golden brown. Turn each potsticker to brown the other side.

7. Reduce the heat to medium, pour the reserved sauce over the potstickers, cover, and cook for 3 minutes. Remove the cover and continue cooking until all the sauce is absorbed.

MAKES 32 POTSTICKERS

Each potsticker contains approximately 29 calories; 3 mg cholesterol; negligible fat; 57 mg sodium.

SPICY SOUTHWESTERN PASTA

This dish is equally tasty made with any pasta cut. However, I like the appearance best when made with rotelle, the little wagon wheels.

1 ½ teaspoons cumin seeds
4 cups tomato puree (two 14-ounce cans)
1 large onion, finely chopped (2 cups)
3 cloves garlic, pressed or minced (1 tablespoon)
¼ teaspoon salt
¼ teaspoon freshly ground black pepper
¼ teaspoon red pepper flakes or to taste
2 teaspoons chili powder
2 teaspoons dried oregano, crushed
One 4-ounce can diced green chilies
One 7-ounce jar roasted red peppers, drained and diced
One 16-ounce can black beans, rinsed and drained
1 ½ cups fresh or frozen corn kernels
½ cup light sour cream
1 pound rotelle, cooked al dente
6 ounces reduced-fat sharp Cheddar cheese, shredded (1 ½ cups)
Chopped cilantro (fresh coriander), for garnish

1. Place a large pot or skillet over medium heat. Add the cumin seeds and toast them, stirring constantly, until a golden brown. Add 3 cups of the tomato puree, the onion, garlic, salt, pepper, pepper flakes, chili powder, and oregano. Mix well and bring to a simmer.

2. Reduce the heat to low and cook, covered, for 25 minutes. Add the remaining tomato puree, the green chilies, red peppers, beans, and corn. Mix well and cook for 5 minutes. Remove ½ cup of the mixture from the pan. Mix it with the sour cream and then add this mixture back to the pan and mix well.

3. To serve, place 1 cup of the cooked pasta on each of eight plates and top each serving with 1 cup sauce. Sprinkle each serving with 3 tablespoons of the grated cheese and as much cilantro as desired.

MAKES 8 SERVINGS

Each serving contains approximately 473 calories; 19 mg cholesterol; 7 g fat; 412 mg sodium.

SPRING VEGETABLE STEW WITH LEMON AND CHIVE NOODLES AND PESTO

Chervil is a mild-flavored member of the parsley family with an elusive anise flavor. It is available dried, but has the best flavor when fresh. Both forms can be found in most supermarkets in the produce section, with the packaged fresh herbs, or in the spice section.

2 pounds fresh fava beans, shelled (1 cup)
1 pound fresh black-eyed peas, shelled (1 cup)
3 cups small broccoli florets
5 cups vegetable stock (see page 15)
12 ounces fresh Lemon and Chive Pasta (see page 223)
1 pound asparagus, tough stems peeled and cut into 2-inch pieces

1 fennel bulb, outer layer removed and cut into 1-inch dice (1 cup)

2 cups fresh garden peas

2 medium tomatoes, peeled, seeded, and cut into 1-inch cubes

1 small yellow squash, sliced into ¼-inch rounds

10 ounces fresh spinach leaves, stems and veins removed, thoroughly washed and drained

⅓ cup finely chopped fresh chervil leaves, or 1 tablespoon dried crushed

2 tablespoons fresh tarragon leaves

½ teaspoon kosher salt

¼ teaspoon freshly ground black pepper

3 tablespoons Pesto Sauce (see page 70), for garnish

1. Bring a large pot of salted water to a boil. Blanch the fava beans for 2 minutes. Remove the beans and plunge into ice water to cool immediately. Drain and discard the outside shell of the bean. In the same boiling water, blanch the black-eyed peas for 1 minute and plunge into the ice water. Continue the same procedure with the broccoli and blanch for 30 seconds. Set the vegetables aside.

2. In a nonreactive pot, bring the vegetable stock to a boil. At the same time bring another pot of salted water to a boil. Add the noodles to the salted water and cook to just al dente, about 2 to 3 minutes. Drain thoroughly and set aside.

3. While the noodles are cooking, add the asparagus and fennel to the boiling vegetable stock and cook for 30 seconds. Add the garden peas, tomatoes, squash, spinach, and blanched beans, black-eyed peas, and broccoli and cook for 3 minutes. Add the chervil, tarragon, salt, pepper, and drained pasta and mix well. Serve immediately in warm soup plates and finish by lacing ½ tablespoon pesto sauce over the top of each serving, for garnish.

Makes six 2-cup servings

Each serving contains approximately 295 calories; 3 mg cholesterol; 3 g fat; 375 mg sodium.

THREE SISTERS CASSEROLE

The American Indians worshipped corn and many of their religious ceremonies centered around its growth cycle, from planting to harvest. They always planted it along with squash, to keep the weeds away, and beans, which could climb the corn stalks for support. They referred to this trio of corn, squash, and beans as the Three Sisters. Many original Indian dishes contain these three ingredients which, in combination, are extremely nutritious and also very tasty.

1 ½ teaspoons cumin seeds
2 large onions, finely chopped (3 cups)
2 cloves garlic, minced
2 carrots, scraped and diced
1 jalapeño pepper, seeded and finely chopped
One 28-ounce can ready-cut tomatoes, undrained
1 ½ cups fresh or frozen corn kernels
3 medium zucchini, diced
8 ounces penne, cooked al dente (4 cups)
One 16-ounce can red kidney beans, rinsed and drained
4 ounces reduced-fat sharp Cheddar cheese, grated (1 cup)

1. Place the cumin seeds in a large nonstick skillet and cook over low heat until you can smell them. Add the onion and garlic and cook, covered, until the onion is soft and translucent, 10 to 15 minutes. Stir occasionally and add a little water or stock, if necessary, to prevent scorching.

2. Add the carrots, jalapeño, and the tomatoes and their juice and simmer, uncovered, for 15 minutes. Add the corn and zucchini and simmer until the zucchini is tender, about 5 more minutes. Stir in the cooked pasta and drained beans and mix well.

3. Preheat the oven to 350°F. Spoon the mixture into a 4-quart casserole or baking dish that has been sprayed with nonstick vegetable

coating. Spread the cheese evenly over the top and bake in the pre-heated oven until the cheese is melted, about 5 minutes.

MAKES ABOUT 12 CUPS, EIGHT 1 ½-CUP SERVINGS

Each serving contains approximately 201 calories; 9 mg cholesterol; 1 g fat; 217 mg sodium.

FUSILLI ARROVIATTA

Arroviatta is a hot and spicy tomato sauce popular in the southern part of Italy. If you don't like hot sauces then just use less of the red pepper flakes. If you really like your pasta "picante," then add a bit more—but taste this sauce first because it's already very spicy! I like it served with a corkscrew-style pasta, like fusilli, because the sauce clings to the grooves.

1 tablespoon olive oil
1 teaspoon red pepper flakes or to taste
2 cloves garlic, pressed or minced
¼ teaspoon freshly ground black pepper
One 28-ounce can ready-cut tomatoes, undrained
½ teaspoon salt
¼ cup packed chopped fresh parsley
1 pound fusilli, cooked al dente
Freshly grated Parmesan cheese, for garnish (optional)

1. Warm the oil in a large skillet over medium heat. Add the red pepper flakes and cook, stirring constantly, until the oil turns slightly red.

2. Add the garlic to the oil mixture and cook just until the garlic sizzles. Add the tomatoes and their juice and the salt and pepper. Mix well and bring to a simmer. Reduce the heat to low and simmer, uncovered, until the sauce has thickened, about 20 minutes. Add the parsley and mix well.

3. Be sure the pasta is drained thoroughly and toss the pasta and sauce together until well combined. Top each serving with grated Parmesan cheese, if desired.

MAKES SIX 1 ½-CUP SERVINGS

Each serving contains approximately 332 calories; no cholesterol; 4 g fat; 422 mg sodium.

SOBA NOODLES WITH PEANUT SAUCE

This oriental pasta dish is served either at room temperature or cold. I like it best at room temperature with cilantro (fresh coriander) leaves as well as scallions for garnish or served on the side.

⅓ cup smooth unhomogenized (old-fashioned) peanut butter
⅓ cup water
2 cloves garlic, quartered
1 tablespoon chopped peeled fresh ginger
2 tablespoons plus 1 teaspoon dark sesame oil
2 tablespoons reduced-sodium soy sauce
2 tablespoons rice vinegar
1 tablespoon sugar
½ teaspoon hot pepper oil
6 scallions, finely chopped (¾ cup)
8 ounces soba noodles

1. In a blender container or food processor, combine the peanut butter, water, garlic, ginger, 2 tablespoons of the sesame oil, the soy sauce, vinegar, sugar, and hot pepper oil. Blend or process until smooth and pour into a mixing bowl. Add ½ cup of the scallions and mix well. Reserve the remaining scallions for garnish.

2. Cook the noodles in 4 quarts of boiling water until just tender, about 3 to 4 minutes. Rinse with cold water and drain well. Toss the noodles with the remaining teaspoon of sesame oil until they are even-

ly coated with the oil. Pour the peanut sauce over the noodles and toss again to mix well.

3. To serve, spoon 1 cup of the mixture onto each of four plates and sprinkle 1 tablespoon of the chopped scallions over the top of each serving.

MAKES ABOUT 4 CUPS, FOUR 1-CUP SERVINGS

Each serving contains approximately 438 calories; no cholesterol; 20 g fat; 701 mg sodium.

SOBA WITH VEGETABLES

4 dried Chinese oyster or shiitake mushrooms
1 ½ teaspoons dark sesame oil
1 ½ teaspoons peanut oil
2 cloves garlic, pressed or minced
1 teaspoon minced peeled fresh ginger
2 small zucchini, cut diagonally into ¼-inch-thick slices
¼ pound Chinese pea pods, ends notched and strings removed
4 ounces soba noodles, cooked according to package instructions and drained
1 tablespoon reduced-sodium soy sauce

1. Soak the dried mushrooms in warm water for 30 minutes. Drain, remove and discard the stems, and cut the caps into thin strips. Set aside.

2. Warm the oil in a wok or a large skillet over medium-high heat. Add the garlic and ginger and stir-fry for 1 minute. Add the sliced mushrooms, zucchini, and pea pods and stir-fry for 1 minute more. Add the soba noodles and stir-fry for 2 minutes. Add the soy sauce and stir-fry for 1 minute. Serve immediately.

MAKES 6 CUPS, FOUR 1 ½-CUP SERVINGS

Each serving contains approximately 160 calories; no cholesterol; 4 g fat; 351 mg sodium.

BOILED WHITE RICE

2 cups water or defatted stock
1 cup white rice

Combine the water and the rice in a saucepan with a tight-fitting lid and bring to a boil over medium heat. Stir, reduce the heat to low and simmer, tightly covered, until all the liquid is absorbed and the rice is tender, about 15 minutes. Fluff with a fork before serving.

MAKES 3 CUPS, SIX ½-CUP SERVINGS

Each serving contains approximately 88 calories, no cholesterol; negligible fat; 162 mg sodium.

BOILED BROWN RICE

2 ¼ cups water or defatted stock
1 cup brown rice

Bring the water to a boil in a saucepan with a tight-fitting lid. Stir in the rice and reduce the heat to low. Simmer, tightly covered, until all the liquid is absorbed and the rice is tender, 45 to 50 minutes. Fluff with a fork before serving.

MAKES 3 CUPS, SIX ½-CUP SERVINGS

Each serving contains approximately 122 calories; no cholesterol; 1 g fat; 182 mg sodium.

BOILED WILD RICE

3 cups water or defatted stock
1 cup (5 ⅓ ounces) wild rice

In a saucepan with a tight-fitting lid, bring the water or stock to a boil over medium-high heat. Stir in the wild rice and reduce the heat to low. Simmer, tightly covered, until the rice kernels burst and are tender, about 45 to 50 minutes. Fluff with a fork before serving.

MAKES ABOUT 4 CUPS, EIGHT ½-CUP SERVINGS

Each serving contains approximately 82 calories; no cholesterol; 1 g fat; 181 mg sodium.

FRIED RICE

2 tablespoons peanut oil
12 scallions, finely chopped (2 cups)
2 cups cooked rice
1 large egg plus 2 egg whites, lightly beaten
2 tablespoons reduced-sodium soy sauce

1. Warm the oil in a nonstick skillet or wok over medium-high heat. Add the scallions and cook, stirring constantly, until lightly browned. Add the rice and mix well.

2. Combine the egg and egg whites with the soy sauce, mix well, and add to the rice mixture. Cook, stirring constantly, until the egg is cooked and the mixture is hot.

MAKES ABOUT 3 CUPS, SIX ½-CUP SERVINGS

Each serving contains approximately 147 calories; 35 mg cholesterol; 5 g fat; 194 mg sodium.

CAJUN RICE

1 cup long-grain white rice
2 cups defatted chicken stock (see page 15)
1/4 teaspoon dried oregano, crushed
1/4 teaspoon dried basil, crushed
1/4 teaspoon salt (omit if using salted stock)
1/8 teaspoon dried thyme, crushed
1/8 teaspoon paprika
Pinch of ground allspice

Combine all ingredients in a saucepan with a tight-fitting lid. Bring to a boil over medium heat, reduce the heat to low and simmer, covered, until the rice is tender and all the liquid is absorbed, about 15 minutes.

MAKES 3 CUPS, SIX ½-CUP SERVINGS

Each serving contains approximately 91 calories; no cholesterol; 0 g fat; 261 mg sodium.

GREEN RICE

1 tablespoon canola oil
1 medium onion, finely chopped (1 1/2 cups)
2 pounds fresh spinach leaves
3 cups cooked brown rice
1/4 cup whole-wheat flour
8 ounces reduced-fat sharp Cheddar cheese, grated (2 cups)
2 1/2 cups nonfat milk
3/4 teaspoon salt
1/4 teaspoon freshly ground black pepper

1. Preheat the oven to 350°F. Place the oil in a skillet over low heat. Add the onion and cook, covered, stirring occasionally, until soft and translucent, 10 to 15 minutes.

2. While the onion is cooking, wash the spinach thoroughly and remove the large stems and veins. Chop the spinach and steam over rapidly boiling water for 1 minute. Squeeze the excess liquid from the spinach and set aside.

3. Combine the rice and flour and mix well. Add the cooked onions, spinach, and cheese, and mix well again. (The recipe may be made ahead to this point and refrigerated until later in the day or even the next day.)

4. Combine the milk, salt, and pepper and add to the rice mixture. Mix well and spoon into an ovenproof casserole. Bake until hot and bubbly, and lightly browned on the top, 1 hour and 15 minutes.

MAKES TWELVE ½-CUP SERVINGS

Each serving contains approximately 163 calories; 17 mg cholesterol; 6 g fat; 263 mg sodium.

BASIC RISOTTO

Unlike other boiled white rice, which should never be stirred while cooking, risotto, made with arborio rice, requires frequent stirring and a slightly longer cooking time.

To make risotto, use a heavy pan, a little oil, butter, or margarine, some garlic, onion, shallots, or other seasonings of your choice. Immediately add the arborio rice and stir well. Then start adding the liquid, ½ cup at a time, stirring frequently, until almost all of the liquid has been absorbed, always leaving a "veil" of liquid over the rice.

Be careful not to get the risotto too dry or it will have a gummy consistency. After the last liquid has been added and the risotto has a creamy texture, remove it from the heat and add a little grated cheese and a small amount of oil, margarine, or butter, to smooth out the texture.

1 tablespoon olive oil
2 tablespoons finely chopped onion
½ cup arborio rice
¼ cup dry white wine
2 ½ cups defatted chicken stock (see page 15)
¼ cup freshly grated Parmesan cheese
½ tablespoon corn-oil margarine

1. Warm the oil in a heavy pot. Add the onion and cook over medium-low heat, stirring constantly, until the onion is translucent, about 5 minutes. Add the rice and mix well.

2. Add the wine and cook, stirring frequently, until almost all the liquid is absorbed. Add the stock, ½ cup at a time, always allowing almost all of it to be absorbed before adding more. Stir frequently.

3. After all of the stock is added, about 20 minutes cooking time, remove from the heat and add the cheese and margarine and mix well. Risotto should have a creamy, cereallike consistency. Serve immediately.

MAKES 3 CUPS, SIX ½-CUP SERVINGS

Each serving contains approximately 118 calories; 3 mg cholesterol; 5 g fat; 271 mg sodium.

Microwave Variation:

1. Place the oil in a deep-sided microwave-safe baking dish and cook at full power for 3 minutes. Add the onion and cook at full power for 2 more minutes.

2. Add the rice and mix well. Cook at full power for 2 minutes. Add the wine and 1 ¼ cups of the stock and cook at full power for 8 minutes. Stir in remaining stock and cook at full power for 8 more minutes.

3. Allow to rest for 3 minutes, then add the cheese and margarine and mix well. Serve immediately.

WILD MUSHROOM RISOTTO

1 ½ cups dried porcini or shiitake mushrooms (1 ½ ounces)
5 cups hot water
1 tablespoon corn-oil margarine
½ cup arborio rice
½ cup plus 4 teaspoons freshly grated Parmesan cheese (about 2 ⅓
*   ounces)*
4 teaspoons very finely chopped fresh Italian parsley, for garnish
4 sprigs Italian parsley, for garnish

1. Place the dried mushrooms in a large bowl and pour the hot water over them. Allow to soak for 30 minutes. Strain through a fine sieve lined with several layers of cheesecloth. Reserve the soaking water to cook the rice. Wash the mushrooms to remove all grit and sand. Cut off any stems, cut into thin strips, and set aside.

2. Pour the reserved strained liquid into a pan and bring to a simmer over low heat.

3. Melt the margarine in a heavy pot over medium heat. Add the rice and stir until each grain of rice is coated and shiny, about 2 minutes. Pour ½ cup of the hot mushroom liquid into the rice and cook, stirring constantly until the liquid is almost absorbed. (There should always be a "veil" of liquid over the top of the rice.) Add the mushrooms and mix well. Continue to add liquid, ½ cup at a time, until the rice is tender and has the texture of cooked cereal, about 20 minutes (the exact amount of liquid needed to make risotto will vary every time you make it).

4. Stir ½ cup of the grated cheese into the rice and stir to blend to a creamy consistency. Serve immediately. To serve, spoon ¾ cup of the rice into each of four au gratin dishes. Top each with 1 teaspoon of grated Parmesan cheese, 1 teaspoon of minced parsley, and a parsley sprig.

MAKES FOUR ¾-CUP SERVINGS

Each serving contains approximately 202 calories; 9 mg cholesterol; 7 g fat;
258 mg sodium.

BRIGHT BEET RISOTTO

✖

Arborio is a wide-grain rice, slightly translucent with a "pearl" of opaque white at its core. It is perfect for making risotto. As it cooks, the translucent exterior dissolves, releasing its creamy starch to the developing sauce. The opaque core becomes tender and slightly chewy. In Venice, this texture is often described as chewy rice floating in a sea of cream. The beets give this particular recipe a billiant color and uniquely different taste.

½ pound beets, peeled and diced (1 ½ cups)
½ cup chopped onion
2 ½ cups defatted chicken stock (see apge 15)
½ teaspoon salt (omit if using salted stock)
¼ teaspoon freshly ground black pepper
¾ teaspoon dried oregano, crushed
½ teaspon dried thyme, crushed
1 tablespoon olive oil
1 clove garlic, minced or pressed
½ cup arborio rice
¼ cup Pernod
1 tablespoon corn-oil margarine
⅓ cup freshly grated Parmesan cheese
Chopped fresh chives, for garnish (optional)

1. Combine the beets, onion, and 1 ½ cups of the chicken stock in a medium-size saucepan. Add the salt, pepper, oregano, and thyme and bring to a boil over medium heat. Reduce the heat to low and cook, covered, for 10 minutes. Remove from the heat and pour the mixture into a blender container. Process until completely smooth, then add the remaining cup of stock and mix well.

2. Heat the oil in a heavy skillet. Add the garlic and cook, stirring, over medium heat just until it sizzles. Add the rice and cook, stirring constantly, for 2 minutes to coat the rice with the oil. Add the Pernod and cook until most of it has been absorbed or evaporated. Add ½ cup of the pureed beet and stock mixture and stir until almost all of it has been absorbed. Repeat this process as you continue adding the beet mixture, ½ cup at a time, stirring frequently, until all of the beet mixture has been added. This takes about 20 minutes. Do not allow the last addition to become completely absorbed or the risotto will be pasty.

3. Remove from the heat and stir in the margarine until well blended. Stir in cheese and mix well. Serve immediately and garnish each serving with a sprinkle of chopped chives and additional grated Parmesan cheese, if desired.

MAKES ABOUT 3 CUPS, SIX ½-CUP SERVINGS

Each serving contains approximately 153 calories; 3 mg cholesterol; 6 g fat; 355 mg sodium.

BIRIYANI
(INDIAN RICE WITH VEGETABLES)

This colorful and aromatic rice dish is very popular in India. It is classically served with yogurt, either on the side or spooned over the top.

1 ½ cups basmati rice (or long-grain white rice)
1 ½ tablespoons peanut oil
½ large onion, finely chopped (¾ cup)
2 cloves garlic, pressed or minced
1 small green bell pepper, seeded, and diced (¾ cup)
4 cardamom pods
4 cloves
6 black peppercorns
1 cinnamon stick, broken in half
2 large Roma tomatoes, diced (1 cup)
1 Japanese eggplant, diced (1 cup)
2 small carrots, scraped and diced (1 cup)
1 cup small cauliflower florets
1 cup frozen peas
2 ½ cups vegetable or defatted chicken stock (see page 20 or 15)
1 teaspoon salt (omit if using salted stock)
¼ teaspoon ground cayenne pepper
Nonfat plain yogurt (optional)

1. Wash the rice, drain thoroughly, and set aside. Place the oil in a 3 ½-quart pan over medium-low heat. Add the onion, garlic, bell pepper, cardamom, cloves, peppercorns, and cinnamon stick and cook, stirring frequently, until the onion is soft and translucent, 5 to 10 minutes.

2. Add the tomatoes and rice, mix well, and continue to cook, stirring frequently, for 5 more minutes. Add the eggplant, carrots, cauliflower, and peas and mix well. Add the stock, salt, and cayenne pepper. Mix well and bring to a boil. Cover and simmer until the rice is tender and the liquid is absorbed, about 20 minutes.

3. To serve, spoon 1 ¼ cups of the rice mixture onto each plate and, if desired, serve with plain nonfat yogurt.

MAKES 10 CUPS, EIGHT 1 ¼-CUP SERVINGS

Each serving contains approximately 200 calories; no cholesterol; 3 g fat; 330 mg sodium.

SHERRIED FRUIT AND RICE DRESSING

½ cup diced dried apricots
½ cup diced dried prunes
⅓ cup dry sherry
¼ cup pine nuts
1 cup nonfat milk
2 cups fresh whole-wheat bread crumbs
2 tablespoons corn-oil margarine
½ cup chopped shallots
½ cup diced celery
2 cups cooked brown rice
¼ cup chopped fresh parsley

1. Preheat the oven to 350°F. Soak the apricots and prunes in the sherry for 15 minutes. While the fruit is soaking, place the pine nuts on a pie plate or baking sheet and toast in the preheated oven until golden brown, 8 to 10 minutes. Watch carefully, they burn easily. Set aside. Reduce the oven temperature to 325°F.

2. Drain the fruit, reserving the sherry. Combine the sherry and milk and pour the mixture over the bread crumbs. Set aside.

3. Melt the margarine in a skillet over medium-low heat. Add the fruit and cook, stirring frequently, for 5 minutes. Add the shallots and celery and continue cooking until the shallots are soft and translucent, 10 to 15 minutes.

4. In a large bowl, combine the rice and parsley, tossing to mix well. Add the bread crumb mixture and cooked fruit mixture and

again toss thoroughly. Spoon into a 1 ½-quart casserole sprayed with nonstick vegetable coating and bake in the preheated 325°F oven until the liquid has been absorbed, the rice and fruit are tender, and the top is a golden brown, about 45 minutes.

MAKES ABOUT 6 CUPS, EIGHT ¾-CUP SERVINGS

Each serving contains approximately 247 calories; 1 mg cholesterol; 7 g fat; 189 mg sodium.

CREAMY RICE AND ZUCCHINI

¼ *cup plain nonfat yogurt*
¼ *cup freshly grated Parmesan cheese*
½ *cup low-fat ricotta cheese*
1 *teaspoon salt*
¼ *teaspoon freshly ground black pepper*
⅛ *teaspoon red pepper flakes*
3 *cups nonfat milk*
1 *cup long-grain white rice*
2 *medium zucchini, julienne cut (2 cups)*

1. Combine the yogurt, Parmesan and ricotta cheeses, salt, pepper, and red pepper flakes in a blender or food processor and blend until smooth. Set aside.

2. Bring the milk to a simmer over medium-low heat. Stir in the rice, reduce the heat and simmer, covered, for 10 minutes. Add the zucchini and continue to simmer, covered, until the rice is tender but not all of the liquid is absorbed, about 10 minutes more.

3. Remove from the heat and stir in the cheese mixture. Serve immediately.

MAKES 4 CUPS, EIGHT ½-CUP SERVINGS

Each serving contains approximately 135 calories; 8 mg cholesterol; 2 g fat; 415 mg sodium.

BROWN RICE AND RAISIN PILAF

½ medium onion, finely chopped (¾ cup)
1 medium carrot, scraped and finely chopped
1 medium rib celery, without leaves, finely chopped
¾ cup brown rice
1 teaspoon dried sage, crushed
1 teaspoon dried thyme, crushed
1 bay leaf
½ teaspoon salt (omit if using salted stock)
¼ teaspoon freshly ground black pepper
½ cup raisins
2 cups defatted chicken or turkey stock (see page 15)

1. Combine the onion, carrot, and celery in a heavy pan and cook, covered, over low heat until the onion is soft and translucent, about 10 minutes. Stir occasionally and add a little water or stock, if necessary, to prevent scorching.

2. Add all remaining ingredients except the stock and mix well. Add the stock and bring to a boil over medium heat. Reduce the heat to low and simmer, covered, until the rice is tender and the liquid is absorbed, 45 to 50 minutes. Add more stock, if necessary, to prevent the rice from getting too dry before it is tender. Remove the bay leaf before serving.

MAKES ABOUT 4 CUPS, EIGHT ½-CUP SERVINGS

Each serving contains approximately 136 calories; no cholesterol; 1 g fat;
372 mg sodium.

MONTEREY ZUCCHINI CASSEROLE

3 cups cooked brown rice
One 4-ounce can diced green chilies
8 ounces reduced-fat Monterey Jack cheese, sliced
3 medium zucchini, sliced into ¼-inch rounds
3 large tomatoes, peeled and thinly sliced
2 tablespoons minced fresh parsley
One 16-ounce container light sour cream (2 cups)
¼ cup seeded and chopped green bell pepper
¼ cup chopped scallions
1 teaspoon dried oregano, crushed
1 teaspoon garlic salt
6 ounces Monterey Jack cheese, shredded (1 ½ cups)

1. Preheat the oven to 350°F. Spray a 9- by 13-inch baking dish with nonstick vegetable coating. Spread the rice in the bottom of the dish. Evenly distribute the green chilies over the rice and the sliced cheese over the chilies. Next layer the zucchini over the cheese and the sliced tomatoes over the zucchini.

2. In a small mixing bowl, combine the parsley, sour cream, green pepper, scallion, oregano, and garlic salt. Mix well and spoon over the tomatoes, spreading to distribute as evenly as possible. Sprinkle the shredded cheese over the top.

3. Bake until hot and bubbly, about 30 minutes. Allow to rest about 5 minutes before serving.

MAKES 8 SERVINGS

Each serving contains approximately 367 calories; 29 mg cholesterol; 17 g fat; 466 mg sodium.

ROASTED CHILE CHEESE CUSTARD WITH RICE AND TOMATOES

Two 7-ounce cans roasted whole chilies
1 large tomato, peeled and diced
½ cup chopped scallions
1 clove garlic, pressed or minced
1 cup cooked brown rice
⅛ teaspoon ground cayenne pepper or to taste
2 large eggs plus 3 egg whites
¾ cup low-fat (2%) milk
½ teaspoon ground cumin
⅛ teaspoon freshly ground black pepper
⅔ cup grated reduced-fat sharp Cheddar cheese

1. Preheat the oven to 375°F. Spray a 7- by 11-inch baking dish with nonstick vegetable coating and dice two of the chilies.

2. In a medium-size bowl, combine the diced chilies, tomato, scallions, garlic, rice, and cayenne pepper and mix well. In a large mixing bowl, whisk together the eggs and egg whites, the milk, cumin, and black pepper.

3. Slit open each remaining whole chili and lay 4 chilies open flat in the bottom of the baking dish. Spoon half of the tomato mixture over the chilies and sprinkle with ⅓ cup of the cheese. Next pour ¾ cup of the milk and egg mixture over the cheese layer.

4. Repeat the layers finishing with the remaining milk and egg mixture. Bake until the custard is a golden brown and puffed, about 30 minutes.

MAKES 4 SERVINGS

Each serving contains approximately 254 calories; 120 mg cholesterol; 8 g fat; 193 mg sodium.

SPINACH SOUFFLÉ PIE

FOR THE CRUST

1 ½ cups cooked brown rice
1 large egg white, lightly beaten
1 tablespoon freshly grated Parmesan cheese

FOR THE FILLING

1 tablespoon corn-oil margarine
2 tablespoons minced onion
2 tablespoons unbleached all-purpose flour
½ teaspoon salt
⅛ teaspoon freshly ground black pepper
1 cup nonfat milk, heated
1 large egg, separated, plus 3 additional egg whites
One 10-ounce package frozen chopped spinach, thawed and well drained
2 ounces reduced-fat Swiss cheese, grated (½ cup)

1. Preheat the oven to 350°F. To make the crust, combine the rice, egg white, and Parmesan cheese and mix well. Spray a 9-inch pie pan with nonstick vegetable coating and spread the rice mixture evenly over the bottom and sides of the pan, pressing lightly with your fingertips or the back of a spoon to shape into a crust. Bake for 5 minutes, then remove from the oven and set aside. Increase the oven temperature to 375°F.

2. To make the filling, melt the margarine in a large saucepan over medium heat, then add the onion and cook until it is soft and transparent. Stir in the flour, salt, and pepper and cook, stirring constantly, for 2 minutes. Remove from the heat and blend in the milk. Return the mixture to the heat and stir constantly until thickened, about 8 minutes. Remove from the heat, add the egg yolk and beat well.

3. Beat the egg whites until stiff but not dry peaks form. Add ¼ cup of the beaten egg whites to the sauce mixture and stir in the

spinach and cheese. Gently fold in the remaining egg whites. Pour the filling into the crust and bake until the egg mixture is set and the top is golden, about 25 minutes.

MAKES ONE 9-INCH PIE, 6 SERVINGS

Each serving contains approximately 171 calories; 43 mg cholesterol; 6 g fat; 350 mg sodium.

WILD RICE AND MUSHROOM QUICHE

One frozen 9-inch pie crust, made with vegetable oil, thawed
1 ½ tablespoons Dijon mustard
1 teaspoon corn-oil margarine
½ pound fresh mushrooms, thinly sliced (2 cups)
4 ounces reduced-fat Monterey Jack cheese, shredded (1 cup)
2 cups cooked wild rice
1 cup low-fat ricotta cheese
½ cup canned evaporated skimmed milk
1 cup liquid egg substitute
¼ teaspoon salt
¼ teaspoon freshly ground black pepper
¼ teaspoon dried marjoram or Italian seasoning, crushed
¼ teaspoon dried thyme, crushed

1. Preheat the oven to 425°F. Line a 9-inch pie pan or quiche dish with the pie crust. Prick the bottom and sides of the crust with a fork. Spread the mustard on the bottom of the pie crust and bake for 7 minutes. Remove the crust from the oven and reduce the temperature to 375°F.

2. Melt the margarine in a medium-size nonstick skillet over medium heat. Add the mushrooms and cook, stirring, just until the

mushrooms are tender. Do not overcook or allow the mushrooms to brown; set aside.

3. Place half the Monterey Jack cheese in the bottom of the partially baked crust. Spread the rice over the cheese and the cooked mushrooms over the rice.

4. In a blender or food processor combine the ricotta cheese, milk, egg substitute, salt, pepper, marjoram, and thyme. Process until smooth and creamy. Pour the egg mixture over the ingredients in the pie shell and top with the remaining Monterey Jack.

5. Place the quiche on a baking sheet and bake at 375°F until a knife inserted in the center comes out clean, about 45 minutes. Allow to rest 5 to 10 minutes before slicing.

MAKES ONE 9-INCH QUICHE, 8 SERVINGS

Each serving contains approximately 295 calories; 10 mg cholesterol; 15 g fat; 448 mg sodium.

QUICK CHILI

3 medium onions, finely chopped (4 ½ cups)
2 cloves garlic, finely chopped (2 teaspoons)
½ cup canned chopped green California chilies, undrained
1 tablespoon chili powder
2 teaspoons dried oregano, crushed
2 teaspoons ground cumin
One 14 ½-ounce can ready-cut tomatoes, drained
2 ½ cups dried kidney beans, cooked (6 cups), or one 46-ounce can,
  undrained

1. Combine the onions and garlic and cook in a large saucepan, covered, over low heat until soft. Stir occasionally and add a little water or stock, if necessary, to prevent scorching.

2. Add all the other ingredients except the beans. Mix thoroughly and bring to a boil over medium heat. Reduce the heat to low and simmer for 10 minutes. Add the cooked beans, mix well, and heat thoroughly.

MAKES 6 CUPS, SIX 1-CUP SERVINGS

Each serving contains approximately 280 calories; no cholesterol; 2 g fat;
100 mg sodium.

WHITE CHILI

This is one of my signature recipes. You can turn it into an entrée by adding cooked chicken just before serving. It is also good with turkey breast, rabbit, veal, or drained water-packed white albacore tuna.

It is important to use a heavy saucepan to cook this. The liquid boils too quickly, even over low heat, in a lightweight pan. If you think you have too much liquid left when the chili has finished cooking, stir it up and let it stand, uncovered, until it cools slightly and much of the liquid will be absorbed. Then reheat to serve.

This chili is a wonderful dish for parties and freezes well.

1 pound dried Great Northern beans, soaked overnight in water to cover and drained
4 cups defatted chicken stock (see page 15)
2 medium onions, coarsely chopped (4 cups)
3 garlic cloves, finely chopped (1 tablespoon)
1 teaspoon salt
½ cup canned chopped green California chilies
2 teaspoons ground cumin
1 ½ teaspoons dried oregano, crushed
1 teaspoon ground coriander
¼ teaspoon ground cloves
¼ teaspoon ground cayenne pepper or to taste
4 ounces pound Monterey Jack cheese, grated (1 cup) (optional)

1. Combine the beans, stock, 2 cups of the onions, the garlic, and salt in a large heavy saucepan or pot and bring to a boil. Reduce the heat, cover, and simmer until the beans are very tender, about 2 hours. Add more stock as needed (more stock should not be needed if you are using a heavy pan or pot).

2. When the beans are tender, add the remaining 2 cups onions, the chilies, and all the seasonings. Mix well and continue to cook, covered, for 30 minutes.

3. To serve, spoon 1 cup chili into each serving bowl and top with 2 tablespoons of Monterey Jack cheese if desired.

MAKES 8 CUPS, EIGHT 1-CUP SERVINGS

Each serving (without cheese) contains approximately 195 calories; no cholesterol; negligible fat; 290 mg sodium.

RED CHILI

1 pound dried red kidney beans, soaked overnight in water to cover
3 cloves garlic, unpeeled
2 teaspoons cumin seeds
2 medium onions, finely chopped (3 cups)
One 4-ounce can chopped California green chilies, undrained
1 tablespoon chili powder
2 teaspoons dried oregano, crushed
One 14-ounce can ready-cut tomatoes, undrained

1. Rinse, drain, and pick over the beans. Place in a large pot and add water to cover by 2 inches. Bring to a boil, reduce the heat and cook, covered, until the beans are tender, about 1 ½ hours.

2. Preheat the oven to 400°F. While the beans are cooking, place the garlic in a pie pan and roast until soft, about 10 minutes. Peel the garlic and mash it with a fork. Set aside.

3. Place the cumin seeds in a heavy pot and cook over medium heat until brown and aromatic, about 2 minutes. Add the mashed roasted garlic and the onions and cook, covered, over low heat until the onion is soft and translucent, about 10 minutes. Stir occasionally and add a little water or stock, if necessary, to prevent scorching. Add the canned chilies, chili powder, and tomatoes. Mix well and simmer for 15 minutes.

4. Drain the cooked beans and add them to the tomato mixture. Mix well and cook, covered, for 15 more minutes.

MAKES 6 CUPS, SIX 1-CUP SERVINGS

Each serving contains approximately 135 calories; no cholesterol; 1 g fat; 279 mg sodium.

BLACK BEAN CHILI

The recipe for this delightfully spicy chili was created for Healthy Choice frozen foods by Patrick McDonnell, the talented director of recipe development for ConAgra. Now you can either buy it frozen or make it yourself.

8 ounces dried black beans, soaked overnight in water to cover
6 cups cold water
2 sprigs fresh thyme, or ½ teaspoon dried, crushed
1 bay leaf
3 cloves garlic, unpeeled
1 tablespoon chili powder
1 tablespoon paprika
1 tablespoon cumin seeds
½ teaspoon ground coriander
¼ teaspoon dried oregano, crushed
¼ teaspoon dried marjoram, crushed
⅛ teaspoon ground cinnamon
⅛ teaspoon ground cayenne pepper
Pinch of ground bay leaf
1 tablespoon olive oil
1 large onion, finely chopped (2 cups)
1 large bell pepper, seeded, and finely chopped
½ cup dry red wine
¼ cup seeded and chopped Texas green chilies
6 Roma tomatoes, peeled and diced
½ teaspoon Tabasco sauce or to taste
1 teaspoon salt

OPTIONAL, FOR GARNISH

Chopped cilantro (fresh coriander)
Chopped scallions
Grated reduced-fat Monterey Jack cheese
Whipped low-fat cream cheese or sour cream

1. Drain, rinse, and pick over the beans. Place the beans and the cold water in a heavy pot. Add the thyme and bay leaf and bring to a boil. Reduce the heat to low and simmer, covered, until the beans are tender, about 1 ½ hours.

2. While the beans are cooking, preheat the oven to 400°F. Place the garlic in a pie pan and roast in the oven until soft, about 10 minutes. Remove from the oven, and peel the garlic and mash it with a fork. Set the garlic aside.

3. In the same pie pan, combine the chili powder, paprika, cumin seeds, coriander, oregano, marjoram, cinnamon, cayenne, and ground bay leaf. Roast the mixture until aromatic and dark brown, about 5 minutes. Set aside.

4. When the beans are tender, remove from the heat and drain, reserving 1 cup of the cooking liquid. Heat the oil in a large pot over high heat. Add the onion and green pepper and cook, stirring frequently, until soft, about 5 minutes. Add the reserved cup of cooking liquid and the wine and bring to a simmer. Add the roasted garlic and herbs, the chilies, and the tomatoes. Mix well and cook, covered, over low heat for 10 minutes. Add the Tabasco sauce and salt and mix well.

5. To serve, spoon the chili into serving bowls and top with chopped cilantro, scallions, grated cheese, and a dollop of light sour cream, if desired.

MAKES EIGHT 1-CUP SERVINGS

Each serving contains approximately 158 calories; no cholesterol; 3 g fat; 318 mg sodium.

CUBAN BLACK BEANS AND RICE

This dish is classically served either over or alongside plain boiled rice. This recipe is also fabulous for red beans and rice. Use red instead of black beans, and mix in 3 cups of cooked rice.

1 pound dried black beans, soaked overnight in water to cover
2 large onions, finely chopped (3 cups)
1 large green bell pepper, seeded and chopped (1 cup)
4 cloves garlic, pressed or minced
2 tablespoons sugar
1 teaspoon dried oregano, crushed
½ teaspoon freshly ground black pepper
¼ teaspoon red pepper flakes
2 bay leaves
1 teaspoon salt
2 tablespoons cider vinegar
2 tablespoons extra virgin olive oil
¼ cup dark rum
Cooked rice

1. Drain the beans and place them in a large pot or soup kettle. Add water to cover by 2 inches. Add 1 ½ cups of the chopped onion and bring to a boil over medium heat. Boil for 10 minutes, then reduce the heat to low and simmer, uncovered, for 1 hour.

2. While the beans are cooking, combine the remaining 1 ½ cups onion, the bell pepper, and garlic in a heavy skillet and cook, covered, over low heat until the onion is soft and translucent, 10 to 15 minutes. Stir occasionally and add a little water or stock, if necessary, to prevent scorching. Remove from the heat and set aside.

3. Remove 3 cups of the cooked beans from the pot and puree. Return the pureed beans to the pot. Combine the onion and bell pepper mixture with the beans in the pot and add the sugar, oregano, pepper, red pepper flakes, and bay leaves. Mix well and simmer for 1 more hour, stirring frequently. If necessary add a little more hot water so the beans are always just covered with liquid and do not dry out.

4. Add the salt and vinegar and simmer for 30 more minutes. Add the oil and rum and simmer for 10 minutes. Serve with or over cooked rice.

MAKES ABOUT 6 CUPS, SIX 1-CUP SERVINGS

Each serving contains approximately 228 calories; no cholesterol; 5 g fat; 574 mg sodium.

SOUTHWESTERN FAVA BEAN STEW

1 pound dried fava beans, soaked overnight in water to cover
1 tablespoon olive oil
2 teaspoons dried oregano, crushed
1 ½ teaspoons ground cumin
1 teaspoon ground coriander
½ teaspoon freshly ground black pepper
¼ teaspoon red pepper flakes
2 large onions, chopped (3 cups)
2 cloves garlic, pressed or minced
1 medium green bell pepper, seeded and diced (1 cup)
One 4-ounce can diced green chilies
One 14 ½-ounce can ready-cut tomatoes
5 cups vegetable or defatted chicken stock (see page 15)
½ teaspoon salt (omit if using salted stock)
¼ cup chopped cilantro (fresh coriander)
Shredded reduced-fat sharp Cheddar cheese or Monterey Jack cheese (optional)

1. Drain the beans and remove the tough outer shell. If this is difficult, follow the instructions on page 12 for the boiling method. Set aside.

2. Warm the oil in a heavy pot or soup kettle over medium heat. Add the oregano, cumin, coriander, pepper, and red pepper flakes and cook, stirring constantly, until browned and very aromatic. Add the onion, garlic, and bell pepper and continue to cook, stirring frequently, until the onion is soft and translucent, about 10 minutes.

3. Stir in the canned chilies and their juice and the tomatoes and their juice and cook for 5 minutes. Add the peeled fava beans and stock and bring to a boil over medium-high heat. Boil for 10 minutes, reduce the heat to low and cook, covered, until the beans are tender, about 1 ½ hours. Add the salt and cilantro and mix well.

4. To serve, divide the stew into serving bowls and top with shredded cheese, if desired.

MAKES 8 CUPS, SIX 1 ⅓-CUP SERVINGS

Each serving contains approximately 182 calories; no cholesterol; 4 g fat; 891 mg sodium.

FRIJOLES MEXICANAS (MEXICAN BEANS)

This recipe makes a lot, but the beans keep beautifully in the refrigerator for several weeks, or they can be frozen for several months.

3 large onions, finely chopped (6 cups)
3 cloves garlic, pressed or minced
1 pound dried pinto beans, soaked in water to cover overnight, rinsed, and drained
¾ teaspoon freshly ground black pepper
2 quarts water
1 ½ pounds fresh Roma tomatoes, diced (3 cups)
1 ½ teaspoons salt
¼ cup chopped cilantro (fresh coriander)
One 7-ounce can diced roasted green chilies
¾ teaspoon ground cumin
2 teaspoons chili powder
1 teaspoon fresh lime juice
10 ounces reduced-fat sharp Cheddar cheese, shredded (2 ½ cups)
Cilantro (fresh coriander) sprigs for garnish (optional)

1. Combine 2 cups of the onions and the garlic in a heavy pot over low heat and cook, covered, until soft and translucent, 10 to 15 minutes. Stir occasionally and add a little water or stock, if necessary, to prevent scorching.

2. Add the beans, pepper, and water to the onion mixture and bring to a boil over medium-high heat. Reduce the heat to low and cook, covered, until the beans are tender, about 1 ½ hours. Allow the beans to cool to room temperature.

3. While the beans are cooking, place the tomatoes in a colander, add the salt, and mix well. Allow to stand and drain for at least one hour. Drain the cooled beans, reserving 1 cup of the cooking liquid. Puree the beans in a blender or food processor adding the reserved bean liquid, as necessary, to blend until smooth. Set aside.

4. In the same heavy pot used for cooking the beans, add the remaining chopped onions and the drained tomatoes and cook, covered, over low heat for 30 minutes, stirring occasionally. Add the pureed beans, cilantro, diced chilies, cumin, and chili powder and mix well. Cook, uncovered, over low heat about 30 minutes or until the desired consistency is reached. The beans should be thick, like a thick pudding, but not dry. Add the lime juice and mix well. Serve hot or allow to cool, cover tightly, and refrigerate or freeze for later use. When reheating it may be necessary to thin the beans with a little water or stock. Reheat over low heat, stirring occaionally, until hot.

5. To serve, spoon ½ cup of the beans onto a plate and top with 2 tablespoons shredded cheese. Garnish with fresh cilantro sprigs, if desired.

MAKES TWENTY ½-CUP SERVINGS

Each serving contains approximately 150 calories; 12 mg cholesterol; 4 g fat; 355 mg sodium.

CHEESY BEAN DIP

One 8-ounce package light cream cheese, softened
One 8-ounce container light sour cream
One 16-ounce can vegetarian refried beans
½ package (2 tablespoons) chili seasoning mix
¼ cup finely chopped onion
6 drops Tabasco sauce
8 ounces reduced-fat Cheddar cheese, grated (2 cups)

1. Preheat the oven to 350°F. Spray a 2-quart casserole or baking dish with nonstick vegetable coating. In a large mixing bowl, combine all of the ingredients, reserving ½ cup of the cheese for topping. Spread in the prepared dish and sprinkle with the reserved cheese.

2. Bake until hot, about 30 minutes. Serve with chips or vegetables.

MAKES 5 CUPS, EIGHTY 1-TABLESPOON SERVINGS

Each serving contains approximately 28 calories; 7 mg cholesterol; 2 g fat; 44 mg sodium.

QUICK AND EASY BEAN DIP

This is a delicious dip for toasted tortilla triangles and vegetables of all types.

One 15-ounce can pinto beans, 2 tablespoons of its liquid reserved
¼ teaspoon salt
¼ teaspoon freshly ground black pepper
¼ teaspoon ground cumin
1 teaspoon chili powder
2 drops Tabasco sauce or to taste
½ medium onion, minced (¾ cup)
1 clove garlic, minced or pressed
One 4-ounce can diced green chilies, drained

1. Combine the beans and reserved liquid, the salt, pepper, cumin, chili powder, and Tabasco in a blender and puree until smooth.

2. In a skillet or saucepan over low heat, cook the onion and garlic, covered, until soft and translucent, 10 to 15 minutes. Stir occasionally and add a little water or stock, if necessary, to prevent scorching. Uncover and continue cooking until lightly browned. Add the chilies and cook 3 minutes more. Add the pureed bean mixture, mix well, and heat to the desired temperature.

MAKES EIGHT   2-TABLESPOON SERVINGS

Each serving contains approximately 50 calories; no cholesterol; negligible fat; 312 mg sodium.

BEANS AND BEER

¾ pound (1 ½ cups) dried pinto beans, soaked overnight in water to cover
1 large onion, finely chopped (1 ½ cups)
2 cloves garlic, pressed or minced
1 cup beer
½ pound Roma tomatoes, diced (2 cups)
1 jalapeño pepper, seeded, and finely chopped
1 teaspoon sugar
1 teaspoon salt
½ teaspoon freshly ground black pepper
½ cup loosely packed cilantro (fresh coriander) leaves

1. Drain and rinse the beans. Place them in a pot and cover with water by at least 3 inches. Bring to a boil over medium-high heat. Reduce the heat to low and cook, covered, until the beans are tender, about 1 hour.

2. Combine the onions and garlic in a heavy pan and cook, covered, over low heat until soft and translucent, about 10 minutes. Add the beans, beer, tomatoes, jalapeño, sugar, salt, and pepper. Simmer, covered, for 30 more minutes.

3. Remove from the heat and allow to cool to room temperature. Add the cilantro and mix well. These beans are best served at room temperature. However, they can be refrigerated and served cold, if desired.

MAKES 6 CUPS, EIGHT ¾-CUP SERVINGS

Each serving contains approximately 165 calories; no cholesterol; 1 g fat; 319 mg sodium.

WINNING SUCCOTASH CASSEROLE

One 16 ½-ounce can baby lima beans, rinsed and drained
One 16 ½-ounce can cream-style corn
One 7-ounce jar roasted red peppers, drained
¾ cup cornmeal
¾ cup unbleached all-purpose flour
¼ cup sugar
1 tablespoon baking powder
¼ teaspoon salt
1 cup buttermilk
3 large egg whites
⅓ cup corn-oil margarine, melted

1. Preheat the oven to 350°F. Combine all the ingredients in a large bowl and mix well.

2. Pour into a 13- by 9-inch baking dish sprayed with nonstick vegetable coating and bake until a golden brown on the top, about 1 hour. Cut into twelve 3- by 4 ¼-inch portions.

MAKES 12 SERVINGS

Each serving contains approximately 189 calories; 1 mg cholesterol; 6 g fat; 524 mg sodium.

Lamb Fricassee with Field Vegetables and Garbanzo Beans(page 221) and
Greek Salad with Sprouted Beans (page 64) and Lemon Couscous (page 68)

Halibut en Papillote (page 141) and Linguine with Caviar (page 129)

Chicken Manicotti (page 159) and Sweet Chicken and Rice Cabbage Rolls (page 175)

*Stir-Fried Range Buffalo Appetizer with Black Bean Sauce and Indian Bread
Sticks (page 201)*

Smoked Turkey and Goat Cheese Lasagna (page 172) and Turkey Lasagna Rolls (page 173)

Bright Beet Risotto (page 98) and Creamy Spinach Pasta with Sun-Dried Tomatoes (page 72)

Best Baked Beans (page 214) and Red Beans and Brown Rice (page 215)

Paad Thai (page 131) and White Fish Curry and Aromatic Yellow Rice (page 143)

ENCHILADAS CON FRIJOLES

12 soft corn tortillas
1 medium onion, chopped (1 ½ cups)
1 clove garlic, pressed or minced
1 cup rinsed and drained canned pinto beans
One 14 ½-ounce can tomato puree (2 cups)
One 4-ounce can diced green chilies
½ teaspoon salt
3 cups canned evaporated skimmed milk
8 ounces reduced-fat Monterey Jack cheese, grated (2 cups)
Cilantro (fresh coriander) for garnish (optional)

1. Preheat the oven to 350°F. Wrap the tortillas tightly in aluminum foil and place in the oven for 15 minutes to soften.

2. While the tortillas are warming, cook the onions and garlic, covered, over low heat until soft and translucent, 10 to 15 minutes. Stir occasionally and add a little water or stock, if necessary, to prevent scorching. Add the beans and cook over medium heat, stirring frequently, for 10 minutes. Add the tomato puree, chilies, and salt and mix well. Simmer, uncovered, for 10 minutes.

3. While the bean mixture is simmering, slowly heat the milk to a simmer. Dip each tortilla in the milk and then spoon ¼ cup of the bean mixture down the center of each tortilla.

4. Roll each tortilla around the filling and place, seam side down, in a glass baking dish that has been sprayed with nonstick vegetable coating. Pour the milk over the top and bake for 20 minutes. Remove from the oven and sprinkle the grated cheese evenly over the top. Return to the oven until the cheese is melted, about another 5 minutes.

5. To serve, place each enchilada on a plate and garnish with cilantro, if desired. This recipe may also be made in individual au gratin dishes.

MAKES 12 SERVINGS

Each serving contains approximately 96 calories; 1 mg cholesterol; 1 g fat; 177 mg sodium.

BLACK BEAN STRUDEL WITH LEMON SAUCE

Phyllo dough is found in the frozen food section of your market, often next to the frozen pie shells. It is easy to work with if you follow the package instructions very carefully.

> One 16-ounce can black beans, drained and rinsed
> ½ teaspoon dried thyme, crushed
> 32 sheets phyllo dough, thawed per package instructions
> Olive oil-flavored nonstick vegetable coating
> 8 fresh chives or scallion tops, blanched in boiling water until limp, and drained
> 1 cup Lemon Sauce (see page 22)
> Sprigs fresh thyme for garnish (optional)

1. Preheat the oven to 375°F. Combine the drained beans and dried thyme in a bowl and mix well.

2. Lay a sheet of phyllo dough on a cutting board and, with scissors or a sharp knife, trim into a 10-inch square. Lightly spray with the olive oil-flavored nonstick vegetable coating. Lay another sheet on top and trim to match. Spray the second sheet. Repeat two more times until you have a stack 4 sheets thick.

3. Place ¼ cup of the beans in the center of the dough, gather the sides into the center to form a "purse" with a ruffled edge, and tie with a blanched chive. Spray the "purse" again with the nonstick coating and place on a nonstick baking sheet or one that has been lined with parchment paper or sprayed with nonstick vegetable coating. Repeat the process with the remaining phyllo dough sheets and beans.

4. Bake in the oven until a golden brown, 8 to 10 minutes. Serve each strudel with 2 tablespoons lemon sauce and garnish with fresh thyme, if desired.

MAKES EIGHT 1-STRUDEL SERVINGS

Each serving (without sauce) contains approximately 320 calories; 29 mg cholesterol; 2 g fat; 446 mg sodium.

VEGETABLE PROTEIN PATTIES

These patties are a delicious vegetarian alternative to hamburgers or any other ground-meat patty. They are much lower in saturated fat than their meat counterparts, and more economical as well.

¼ cup chopped almonds
1 cup cooked brown rice
1 cup cooked lentils
1 tablespoon reduced-sodium soy sauce
1 teaspoon dried oregano, crushed
¾ teaspoon dried thyme, crushed
¼ teaspoon freshly ground black pepper
⅛ teaspoon ground cayenne pepper or to taste
½ cup grated carrot (1 carrot)
1 cup rolled (old-fashioned) oats

1. Preheat the oven to 350°F. On an ungreased baking sheet or in a pie pan, toast the almonds in the oven until a deep golden brown, 8 to 10 minutes. Watch carefully, as they burn easily. Set aside.

2. Combine the rice, lentils, soy sauce, oregano, thyme, black pepper, and cayenne in a food processor and mix until smooth. Place the mixture in a bowl and add the carrot, oats, and toasted almonds; mix thoroughly.

3. Form the mixture into eight ¼-cup patties. Spray a skillet with a nonstick vegetable coating and warm over medium-high heat until a drop of water dances on the surface before evaporating. Cook the patties until lightly browned on both sides.

MAKES 8 PATTIES

Each patty contains approximately 124 calories; no cholesterol; 3 g fat; 37 mg sodium.

YELLOW LENTILS WITH MUSTARD GREENS

½ cup chopped onion
½ cup chopped celery
1 clove garlic, pressed or minced
1 jalapeño pepper, seeded, and chopped
½ teaspoon ground cumin
½ teaspoon salt (omit if using salted stock)
¼ teaspoon freshly ground black pepper
¾ cup dried yellow lentils, rinsed and drained
3 cups defatted chicken stock (see page 15)
8 ounces mustard greens, thoroughly washed, stems removed, leaves and
   cut into very thin strips

1. Combine the onion, celery, garlic, jalapeño, cumin, salt, and pepper in a saucepan and cook, covered, over low heat until the onion is soft, about 10 minutes. Stir occasionally and add a little water or stock, if necessary, to prevent scorching. Add the lentils and stock and bring to a boil over medium-high heat.

2. Reduce the heat to low and simmer, covered, until the lentils are tender, but not mushy, 30 to 40 minutes. Stir in the greens and cook, uncovered, for 2 minutes more.

MAKES ABOUT 3 CUPS, FOUR ¾-CUP SERVINGS

Each serving contains approximately 181 calories; negligible cholesterol;
1 g fat; 686 mg sodium.

LEBANESE LENTILS AND BULGUR

1 cup dried lentils, soaked overnight in water to cover
¾ cup bulgur (cracked wheat)
2 large onions, thinly sliced (4 cups)
4 cloves garlic, pressed or minced
1 ½ cups defatted chicken stock (see page 15)
1 tablespoon olive oil

1. Drain and rinse the lentils and set aside. Cover the bulgur with hot water and allow to stand for 15 minutes. Drain well and set aside.

2. Combine 2 cups of the sliced onion and the garlic in a heavy pan and cook over low heat, covered, until the onion is soft and translucent, about 10 to 15 minutes. Stir occasionally and add a little water or stock, if necessary, to prevent scorching. Add the drained lentils, bulgur, and stock and mix well. Bring to a boil over medium heat. Reduce the heat to low and simmer, uncovered, until all liquid is absorbed, about 20 minutes.

3. Warm the oil in a skillet over medium heat. Add the remaining 2 cups onion and stir-fry until the onion is lightly browned.

4. To serve, place about 1 cup of the cooked lentil mixture on each of four plates and top with some of the browned onion.

MAKES ABOUT 4 CUPS, FOUR 1-CUP SERVINGS

Each serving contains approximately 205 calories; 0 mg cholesterol; 4 g fat; 190 mg sodium.

LENTILS AU GRATIN

This is a recipe that I originally developed for the Canyon Ranch Fitness Resorts. It is still one of my favorite lentil dishes.

2 cloves garlic, pressed or minced
2 large onions, finely chopped (3 cups)
6 small carrots (12 ounces), scraped and grated (3 cups)
One 14 ½-ounce can ready-cut tomatoes, drained
1 cup seeded and chopped green bell pepper
5 ⅓ cups cooked lentils (1 ¾ cups dried)
1 teaspoon salt
½ teaspoon freshly ground black pepper
½ teaspoon dried marjoram, crushed
4 ounces reduced-fat Monterey Jack cheese, grated (1 cup)

1. Preheat the oven to 350°F. In a large, heavy saucepan, cook the onions and garlic, covered, over low heat until soft and translucent, 10 to 15 minutes. Stir occasionally and add a little water or stock, if necessary, to prevent scorching.

2. Add the remaining ingredients, except the cheese, and mix well. Spoon the mixture into a 2-quart baking dish that has been sprayed with nonstick vegetable coating. Cover and bake in the preheated oven for 1 hour.

3. To serve, spoon 1 cup of the lentil mixture into individual dishes and sprinkle with 2 tablespoons of the grated cheese. If desired, place the individual servings under a preheated broiler just until the cheese is melted and bubbly.

MAKES ABOUT 8 CUPS, EIGHT 1-CUP SERVINGS

Each serving contains approximately 235 calories; 10 mg cholesterol; 4 g fat;
355 mg sodium.

MIDDLE EASTERN LENTILS AND RICE WITH BROWNED ONIONS

This tasty vegetarian dish is often called "the meat of the poor" in the Middle East. It is traditionally served with bread and yogurt. It is also good cold, and leftovers make a wonderful filling for pita pocket sandwiches.

3 tablespoons olive oil
2 large onions, finely chopped (3 cups)
4 cloves garlic, minced or pressed
¾ teaspoon salt
¾ teaspoon ground cinnamon
¾ teaspoon ground allspice
2 cups dried lentils, rinsed and drained
½ cup long-grain brown rice, rinsed and drained
4 ½ cups water
2 large onions, thinly sliced vertically
3 cups plain nonfat yogurt

1. Heat 2 tablespoons of the oil in a large heavy pot. Add the chopped onions, garlic, salt, cinnamon, and allspice and cook over medium heat, stirring frequently, until the onion is soft and translucent, about 10 minutes.

2. Add the drained lentils and rice and continue to cook, stirring, for 5 more minutes. Add the water and bring to a boil. Cover, and cook over low heat until the liquid is absorbed and the rice is tender, about 1 hour.

3. While the lentil mixture is cooking, heat the remaining tablespoon oil in a large skillet and cook the sliced onions over medium heat, stirring frequently, until the onions are very brown but not scorched.

4. To serve, spoon the lentil and rice mixture onto a serving plat-
ter and cover with a blanket of browned onions. Serve with the
yogurt.

MAKES 9 CUPS, SIX 1 ⅓-CUP SERVINGS

*Each serving contains approximately 469 calories; 2 mg cholesterol; 8 g fat;
396 mg sodium.*

FISH AND SEAFOOD

LINGUINE WITH CAVIAR

I love caviar on anything, but this combination of caviar with the classic condiments and pasta is a real winner. It's not only tasty, but a conversation piece as well!

12 ounces black linguine
1 tablespoon extra virgin olive oil
½ cup reduced-fat sour cream
1 teaspoon lemon zest, plus extra for garnishing
2 tablespoons fresh lemon juice
½ teaspoon salt
¼ teaspoon freshly ground black pepper
2 tablespoons finely chopped fresh chives (optional)
2 ounces caviar (the best your budget will allow)
Extra lemon zest and chopped chives, for garnish (optional)

1. Cook the pasta al dente according to the package instructions, or see page . Drain thoroughly and toss with the oil.

2. While the pasta is cooking, in a medium-size bowl, combine the sour cream with the lemon zest, lemon juice, salt, pepper, and chives. Mix well and fold in the caviar.

3. To serve, pour the sauce over the pasta and toss to mix evenly. Place 1 cup of pasta on each of four plates and garnish with lemon zest and chives, if desired.

MAKES 4 CUPS, FOUR 1-CUP SERVINGS

Each serving contains approximately 357 calories; 150 mg cholesterol; 10 g fat; 564 mg sodium.

HEARTY SEAFOOD PASTA

This gutsy seafood dish dates back to the early days in California when the Italian immigrants made seafood stew with the fish or shellfish available combined with their own "old world" sauces and pasta.

2 onions, finely chopped (3 cups)
3 cloves garlic, minced or pressed
1 large green bell pepper, seeded and diced (2 cups)
½ cup chopped fresh parsley
½ pound Roma tomatoes, peeled and diced, or one 14 ½-ounce can ready-cut tomatoes
One 14 ½-ounce can tomato puree
One 8-ounce can tomato sauce
1 cup dry red wine
½ cup water
1 teaspoon salt
½ teaspoon freshly ground black pepper
¼ teaspoon dried thyme, crushed
¼ teaspoon dried rosemary, crushed
1 pound raw shrimp, shelled and deveined (2 cups)

1 pound sea scallops
1 ½ pounds pasta shells, cooked al dente (12 cups)
2 tablespoons extra virgin olive oil
8 clams, steamed open, for garnish (optional)
8 mussels, steamed open, for garnish (optional)

1. In a heavy pot combine the onion, garlic, and bell pepper and cook, covered, over low heat until soft, about 15 to 20 minutes. Stir occasionally and add a little water, if necessary, to prevent scorching.

2. Add the parsley, tomatoes, tomato puree, tomato sauce, wine, water, salt, pepper, thyme, and rosemary. Mix well and bring to a boil. Reduce the heat to low and cook, covered, for 1 hour, stirring occasionally.

3. Add the seafood to the pot, return to a boil, cover and remove from the heat. Allow to stand for 10 minutes.

4. Drain the cooked pasta thoroughly and toss with the oil. To serve, either mix the pasta with the sauce or serve the sauce over the pasta. Garnish with steamed clams and mussels, if desired.

MAKES 8 SERVINGS, 12 CUPS PASTA AND 10 CUPS SAUCE

Each serving contains approximately 550 calories; 143 mg cholesterol; 7 g fat; 734 mg sodium.

PAAD THAI

Paad Thai is the most popular noodle dish served by the street vendors in Bangkok. It is a country dish which is always made with rice noodles.

8 ounces flat rice sticks, soaked 30 minutes in warm water
2 tablespoons canola oil
3 scallions
2 red chilies, seeded and finely chopped
1 tablespoon finely chopped peeled fresh ginger
4 cloves garlic, pressed or minced
3 tablespoons fish sauce (nam pla)
3 tablespoons rice vinegar
1 tablespoon sugar
12 ounces medium-size shrimp, peeled and deveined
1 large egg, lightly beaten
2 cups fresh mung bean sprouts
¼ cup chopped peanuts
1 lime, quartered, for garnish

1. Cook the noodles in 4 quarts of boiling water until tender, about 1 minute. Drain, toss with 2 teaspoons of the oil, and set aside.

2. Chop the green part of one of the scallions and set it aside for garnish. Finely chop the rest of the scallions and set aside.

3. Place a wok or a large skillet over medium-high heat. Add the remaining 4 teaspoons oil and the chilies and stir-fry for 30 seconds. Add the ginger, garlic, and scallions and stir-fry until tender; do not brown. Add the fish sauce, vinegar, and sugar and mix well. Add the shrimp and cook just until the shrimp become opaque and turn pink.

4. Make a well in the center of the ingredients and pour in the egg. When it starts to set, stir to scramble and toss with the other ingredients. Add the rice sticks and bean sprouts and toss to mix well. Cook just until the bean sprouts start to wilt. Transfer the mixture to a serving dish and sprinkle with the peanuts. Garnish with the reserved chopped scallion top and lime quarters.

MAKES 12 CUPS, SIX 2-CUP SERVINGS

Each serving contains approximately 318 calories; 146 mg cholesterol; 9 g fat; 741 mg sodium.

BROWNED EGGPLANT, PENNE, AND TOMATO-CLAM SAUCE

One 28-ounce can ready-cut tomatoes, undrained
2 cloves garlic, pressed or minced
¾ teaspoon salt
½ teaspoon sugar
1 tablespoon finely chopped fresh basil, or 1 teaspoon dried, crushed
One 7 ½-ounce jar chopped clams, undrained
2 tablespoons olive oil
1 small eggplant, peeled and cut lengthwise in ¼-inch slices
8 ounces penne, cooked al dente (4 cups)
½ cup freshly grated Parmesan cheese

1. Combine the tomatoes, half of the garlic, the salt, sugar, and basil in a 2-quart saucepan. Bring to a boil over medium heat then reduce the heat to low and simmer, uncovered, for 20 minutes, stirring frequently. Remove from the heat, add the clams and their juice, and mix well.

2. While the sauce is simmering, heat the oil in a large skillet over medium heat. Add the remaining garlic and cook until the garlic starts to sizzle. Add the eggplant slices and brown on both sides, then drain on paper towels.

3. To serve, place 1 cup of pasta on each of four warm plates. Pour ¾ cup sauce over each serving and divide the browned eggplant slices evenly among each serving, laying them over the top of the sauce. Sprinkle each serving with 2 tablespoons of the Parmesan cheese. Pass any remaining sauce, if any, as desired.

MAKES 4 SERVINGS

Each serving contains approximately 402 calories; 85 mg cholesterol; 13 g fat;
720 mg sodium.

GREEK SQUID AND ORZO

1 medium-size onion, finely chopped (1 ½ cups)
4 cloves garlic, pressed or minced
¼ cup dry white wine
One 28-ounce can ready-cut tomatoes
¼ cup chopped fresh parsley
6 pitted black olives, finely chopped (2 tablespoons)
½ teaspoon dried basil, crushed
½ teaspoon dried oregano, crushed
½ teaspoon salt
¼ teaspoon freshly ground black pepper
⅛ teaspoon red pepper flakes
1 pound squid, cleaned and diced
1 cup orzo, cooked al dente
2 ounces feta cheese, crumbled (½ cup)

1. Combine the onion and garlic in a heavy pan and cook, covered, over low heat until the onion is soft and translucent, 10 to 15 minutes. Stir occasionally and add a little water or stock, if necessary, to prevent scorching. Add the wine and simmer for 2 minutes.

2. Preheat the oven to 400°F. Add the tomatoes plus their juice to the onion mixture along with 2 tablespoons of the chopped parsley, the olives, basil, oregano, salt, pepper, and red pepper flakes. Cook, stirring occasionally, for 10 minutes. Add the squid and cook until the squid is opaque, 2 to 3 minutes.

3. Place the cooked orzo into a 2-quart casserole dish. Pour in the tomato-squid mixture and mix well. Top with the remaining 2 tablespoons of parsley and sprinkle with the feta cheese. Bake in the preheated oven until the cheese is melted and bubbly, about 10 minutes.

MAKES ABOUT 8 CUPS, SIX 1 ⅓-CUP SERVINGS

Each serving contains approximately 223 calories; 185 mg cholesterol; 4 g fat; 387 mg sodium.

PENNE WITH SHRIMP AND RED BELL PEPPER SAUCE

1 pound medium-size shrimp, peeled and deveined, shells reserved
One 28-ounce can ready-cut tomatoes, undrained
1 cup dry white wine
2 bay leaves
½ teaspoon dried thyme, crushed
½ teaspoon salt
¼ teaspoon freshly ground black pepper
3 teaspoons olive oil
2 medium red bell peppers, seeded, and finely chopped
2 cloves garlic, pressed or minced
2 shallots, minced
½ cup chopped scallions
½ cup loosely packed chopped fresh Italian parsley
1 teaspoon dried basil, crushed
¼ teaspoon red pepper flakes
1 pound penne, cooked al dente (8 cups)
Italian parsley, for garnish (optional)

1. Place the reserved shells from peeling the shrimp in a 2-quart saucepan. Drain the juice from the tomatoes into the saucepan and add the wine and enough water to cover the shells completely. Add 1 bay leaf, the dried thyme, salt, and pepper. Bring to a boil over medium heat and allow to boil until reduced to 1 cup liquid volume. Strain out the solids and set the liquid aside. Discard the solids.

2. Heat 1 ½ teaspoons of the oil in a medium-size nonstick skillet. Cook the red bell pepper over medium-high heat until caramelized, or a brown-black color. Transfer the peppers to a large saucepan and set aside.

3. In the same nonstick skillet, heat the remaining 1 ½ teaspoons oil and cook the garlic, shallots, scallions, and parsley, just until the scallions are soft, about 5 minutes. Add this mixture to the red peppers.

4. Combine the drained tomatoes, remaining bay leaf, basil, and red pepper flakes and add to the red bell pepper mixture. Simmer over medium heat until hot, about 5 minutes. Allow to cool slightly, pour into a food processor or blender container, and process until smooth. Return to the saucepan and bring back to a simmer. Cook the shrimp in the sauce just until they turn from translucent to opaque, or about 2 minutes. Do not overcook.

5. To serve, place 2 cups cooked penne on each of four warm plates. Cover each serving with 1 cup of the sauce and divide the shrimp equally among each serving. Garnish with Italian parsley, if desired.

MAKES 4 SERVINGS

Each serving contains approximately 364 calories; 221 mg cholesterol; 6 g fat; 579 mg sodium.

JOHN DORY, BRAISED ARTICHOKES, AND ROASTED PEPPERS

John Dory is a sweet white fish popular with many people who don't particularly like other fish.

1 teaspoon olive oil
1 clove garlic, minced
1 shallot, minced
1 ½ pounds John Dory fillets
4 artichoke hearts, blanched
1 small fennel bulb, sliced and blanched
2 cups defatted chicken stock (see page 15)
1 cup V-8 juice
1 tablespoon chopped fresh basil
1 tablespoon chopped fresh oregano or 1 teaspoon dried, crushed

½ cup dry white wine
½ teaspoon salt (omit if using salted stock)
¼ teaspoon freshly ground black pepper
2 cups orzo, cooked al dente
¼ cup store-bought roasted red bell peppers (1 ounce)
¼ cup store-bought roasted yellow bell peppers (1 ounce)
1 cup peeled and sliced Roma tomatoes, warmed
4 fresh tarragon sprigs

1. In a heavy pot combine the oil, garlic, and shallot and cook, stirring, over low heat until soft, about 5 minutes. Add the fish, artichokes, fennel, stock, V-8, basil, oregano, wine, salt, and pepper, and simmer slowly, covered, over low heat until the fish turns from translucent to opaque, about 10 minutes.

2. To serve, place ½ cup of the orzo in the bottom of each of four soup plates. Divide the fish evenly among each serving, placing the fish on top of the pasta. Ladle the liquid and vegetables over the fish. Garnish with roasted peppers, warm tomato and a sprig of fresh tarragon.

MAKES 4 SERVINGS

Each serving contains approximately 410 calories; 97 mg cholesterol; 4 g fat; 893 mg sodium.

ROTINI WITH BASIL-ANCHOVY SAUCE

1 cup packed fresh basil leaves
1 cup packed fresh parsley leaves
1 scallion, chopped
3 cloves garlic
1 tablespoon anchovy paste
3 tablespoons fresh lemon juice
½ cup freshly grated Parmesan cheese
3 tablespoons extra virgin olive oil
2 tablespoons water
1 pound rotini, cooked al dente
3 zucchini, grated (3 cups)

1. Combine the basil, parsley, scallion, garlic, anchovy paste, lemon juice, and Parmesan cheese in a food processor and process until smooth. Continue to process while slowly adding the oil and water.

2. Toss the cooked pasta with the grated zucchini and the processed sauce mixture and serve immediately.

MAKES 6 SERVINGS

Each serving contains approximately 404 calories; 5 mg cholesterol; 10 g fat; 160 mg sodium.

SEA BASS AND MEDITERRANEAN VEGETABLES

¼ cup extra virgin olive oil
8 cloves garlic, sliced
2 cups quartered and thinly sliced eggplant

2 cups thinly sliced zucchini
½ teaspoon salt
½ teaspoon freshly ground black pepper
3 cups seeded and diced Roma tomatoes
½ teaspoon orange zest
⅛ teaspoon saffron
¼ teaspoon red pepper flakes
¼ teaspoon dried thyme, crushed
¼ teaspoon dried rosemary, crushed
2 tablespoons chopped fresh parsley
Six 5- to 6-ounce sea bass fillets
12 ounces pasta shells, cooked al dente (6 cups)

1. Heat the oil in a large skillet over medium heat. Add the garlic and cook until a golden brown. Add the eggplant, zucchini, and ¼ teaspoon each of the salt and pepper. Cook, stirring frequently, until the vegetables begin to get tender. Add the tomatoes, orange zest, saffron, red pepper flakes, thyme, rosemary, and parsley and cook for 5 more minutes.

2. Sprinkle the remaining salt and pepper on the fish fillets. Layer half of the cooked vegetables in the bottom of a casserole or baking dish. Place the fish fillets evenly over the top of the vegetables, overlapping them if necessary. Layer the remaining vegetables over the top. Cover and place in a cold oven. Turn the oven to 425°F and cook for 30 minutes.

3. To serve, place 1 cup pasta shells on each of six warm plates. Spoon the fish and vegetables over the cooked pasta.

MAKES 6 SERVINGS

Each serving contains approximately 455 calories; 78 mg cholesterol; 12 g fat; 305 mg sodium.

TUNA AND NOODLE CASSEROLE

1 tablespoon corn-oil margarine
3 tablespoons unbleached all-purpose flour
2 ½ cups nonfat milk, at a simmer
¼ teaspoon salt
¼ teaspoon freshly ground black pepper
¼ teaspoon ground cayenne pepper
4 ounces reduced-fat sharp Cheddar cheese, shredded (1 cup)
One 6 ½-ounce can water-packed solid white tuna, drained and flaked
8 ounces noodles, cooked al dente
¾ cup fresh whole-wheat bread crumbs

1. Preheat the oven to 350°F. Melt the margarine in a heavy saucepan over low heat. Add the flour and cook, stirring, for 2 minutes; do not brown.

2. Remove the pan from the heat and add the simmering milk, stirring constantly with a wire whisk. Add the salt, pepper, and cayenne. Return the pan to the heat and simmer, slowly, until thickened, 15 to 20 minutes, stirring occasionally.

3. Remove the pan from the heat and add the cheese. Mix well and set the sauce aside.

4. Spray a 2-quart casserole with a nonstick vegetable coating. Add the tuna and cooked noodles and toss well. Add the cheese sauce and mix well. Top with the bread crumbs and spray lightly with the vegetable coating. Bake in the preheated oven until bubbly and lightly browned on the top, 20 to 30 minutes.

MAKES ABOUT 6 CUPS, SIX 1-CUP SERVINGS

Each serving contains approximately 335 calories; 59 mg cholesterol; 8 g fat; 427 mg sodium.

HALIBUT EN PAPILLOTE

This is a wonderful recipe for company. You can prepare it ahead of time and keep it in the refrigerator until your guests arrive. Then you heat the sauce, bake the fish, and look like a world-class chef.

FOR THE SAUCE

1 ½ cups coarsely chopped fresh fennel, including fern (6 ounces)
1 ½ cups coarsely chopped onion (6 ounces)
2 cloves garlic
2 tablespoons Pernod
¼ teaspoon fennel seeds
2 tablespoons extra virgin olive oil

FOR THE COUSCOUS

1 ½ cups water
½ teaspoon salt
¼ teaspoon freshly ground black pepper
¼ teaspoon ground allspice
2 teaspoons extra virgin olive oil
1 bay leaf
1 cup (6 ⅔ ounces) couscous

TO ASSEMBLE

4 sheets parchment paper
2 small zucchini, julienne cut (2 cups)
1 pound fresh halibut, cut into four 4-ounce pieces
4 Roma tomatoes, peeled and diced (1 cup)
8 black olives, diced (about 8 teaspoons)
4 teaspoons EACH fresh chopped basil, thyme, and tarragon OR ¼ teaspoon EACH of the dried herbs, crushed
4 teaspoons EACH chopped fresh parsley and chives
1 egg, lightly beaten (for sealing edges of paper)

1. Preheat the oven to 350°F. Combine all the sauce ingredients, except the oil, in a blender and blend until smooth. Pour the mixture into a saucepan and bring to a boil. Pour through a strainer, pressing it through with the back of a spoon to remove all of the liquid. Whisk in the oil, cover, and set aside to keep warm. Makes 1 cup of sauce.

2. To make the couscous, combine the water, salt, pepper, oil, and bay leaf in a sauce pan and bring to a boil. Add the couscous, mix well, remove from the heat and cover. Allow to stand for 5 minutes or until all of the liquid is absorbed.

3. Make 4 large hearts with the parchment paper by folding each piece of paper in half and cutting it into a heart shape. Remove the bay leaf from the couscous, unfold the hearts, and spoon ½ cup couscous onto one side of each of the hearts. Layer with ½ cup of the zucchini, a piece of halibut, ¼ cup of the tomato, about 2 teaspoons diced olives, and 1 teaspoon EACH of the chopped fresh herbs.

4. Rub the outer edges of the paper with the egg and seal the hearts by folding the top half of each heart carefully over the contents, press together the edges, fold the edges over, and crimp them tightly with your fingers. Place the packages on baking sheets and bake for 12 minutes in the preheated oven.

5. To serve, place each package on a large plate and cut an "X" in the top. Fold the four corners back and spoon 2 tablespoons of the sauce over each serving.

MAKES 4 SERVINGS

Each serving contains approximately 400 calories; 35 mg cholesterol; 13 g fat; 478 mg sodium.

WHITE FISH CURRY AND AROMATIC YELLOW RICE

This recipe is based on a Sri Lankan dish I learned from Felicia Sorenson when she was the guest chef at the Robert Mondavi Winery for one of their Great Chef's Weekends.

1 ½ *cups basmati rice*
1 ½ *tablespoons peanut oil*
10 *shallots, thinly sliced (1 ¼ cups)*
6 *cardamom pods or ½ teaspoon ground cardamom*
6 *cloves*
6 *black peppercorns*
1 *teaspoon turmeric*
2 *teaspoons salt*
Two 2-inch pieces lemon grass, pounded
2 *cinnamon sticks, broken in half*
1 ¾ *cups defatted chicken stock (see page 15), hot*
¾ *cup nonfat milk, hot*
3 *teaspoons coconut extract*
1 ½ *pounds firm white fish*
3 *tablespoons fresh lime juice*
¾ *cup water*
1 *serrano chile, seeded and sliced, or to taste*
3 *cloves garlic, sliced*
½ *teaspoon dried fenugreek (available in Indian markets)*
One 12-ounce can low-fat evaporated milk (1 ½ cups)

1. Wash and drain the rice; set aside. Heat the oil in a large saucepan. Add ½ cup of the shallots, the cardamom, cloves, and peppercorns and cook, stirring constantly, until the shallots are soft and transparent; do not brown.

2. Add the rice, ¾ teaspoon of the turmeric, and 1 teaspoon of the salt, one 2-inch piece of the pounded lemon grass, and 1 cinnamon

stick and continue stirring for 3 more minutes. Add the hot stock, the nonfat milk, and 1 ½ teaspoons of the coconut extract and bring to a simmer. Cook, covered, over very low heat for 20 minutes. Do not uncover while cooking. Remove from the heat and do not uncover for 10 more minutes.

3. While the rice is cooking, wash the fish, pat dry, and cut into 1 ½-inch pieces. Combine the lime juice, remaining teaspoon salt, and remaining ¼ teaspoon turmeric and mix well and pour over the fish, tossing to mix well. Set aside.

4. Combine the water, remaining ¾ cup shallots, the serrano chile, garlic, remaining lemon grass and cinnamon stick, and the fenugreek in a large pan and bring to a boil. Boil for 5 minutes to infuse the flavors into the water. Add the canned evaporated milk and remaining 1 ½ teaspoons of coconut extract and bring to a simmer over low heat. Add the fish and continue to simmer until the fish has turned from translucent to opaque. Do not overcook.

5. When the rice is cooked, the spices will rise to the top. Uncover and remove the spices used for flavoring the rice, then fluff the rice with a fork. To serve, measure 1 cup rice onto each of six warm plates. Spread the rice away from the center to make a ring of rice on each plate and spoon ¾ cup of the fish mixture into the center.

MAKES 6 CUPS RICE AND 4 ½-CUPS OF CURRY, 6 SERVINGS

Each serving contains approximately 241 calories; 51 mg cholesterol; 3 g fat; 1068 mg sodium.

"RISOTTO" WITH SHRIMP AND MUSHROOMS

Classic risotto is always made with arborio rice from the Po Valley region in northern Italy. The ratio of liquid to rice is much greater than for other rice varieties, but only a little of the liquid is added at a time and then cooked down before more is added. It is this technique that achieves the creamy consistency characteristic of this rice dish. This "risotto" is a remarkable impostor. It is almost as creamy, higher in fiber, and takes less time to make than the classic risotto. The recipe calls for shrimp, but any other seafood can be substituted. For a delicious vegetarian dish, omit the shrimp and add some colorful cooked vegetables.

2 ounces dried shiitake mushrooms (4 cups)
2 tablespoons extra virgin olive oil
1 medium onion, finely chopped (1 ½ cups)
1 clove garlic, pressed
1 tablespoon fresh basil or 1 teaspoon dried, crushed
1 cup short-grain brown rice
2 ½ cups boiling water
1 ½ cups nonfat milk
1 tablespoon Cream of Rice cereal
½ teaspoon salt
⅛ teaspoon freshly ground black pepper
½ cup freshly grated Parmesan cheese, preferably imported
¼ pound bay shrimp, cooked (1 cup)

1. Soak the mushrooms, stems down, in lukewarm water for 20 to 30 minutes. While the mushrooms are soaking, warm the oil in a saucepan over medium heat. Add the onion, garlic, and basil and cook, stirring frequently, until the onion is soft, about 10 minutes. Add the rice and stir to combine. Add the boiling water and mix well. Cover and cook until the liquid is absorbed, 30 to 40 minutes.

2. Drain the mushrooms and remove and discard the stems. Slice the caps into very thin strips and set aside.

3. Bring the milk to a boil over medium heat. Add the Cream of Rice, salt, pepper, and Parmesan cheese. Cook, stirring, for 30 seconds. Remove from the heat, cover, and allow to stand for 5 minutes. Pour into a blender container and blend until smooth.

4. To the cooked rice add the reserved mushrooms, the cheese mixture, and shrimp; mix well.

MAKES 5 CUPS, FOUR 1 ¼-CUP SERVINGS

Each serving contains approximately 421 calories; 52 mg cholesterol; 12 g fat; 559 mg sodium.

JAMBALAYA

2 cups defatted chicken stock (see page 15)
1 bay leaf
½ teaspoon dried thyme, crushed
1 cup long-grain white rice
1 large onion, finely chopped (1 ½ cups)
1 small green bell pepper, seeded and finely chopped (¾ cup)
1 clove garlic, pressed or minced
One 14 ½-ounce can ready-cut tomatoes, undrained
½ teaspoon salt (omit if using salted stock)
¼ teaspoon freshly ground white pepper
¼ teaspoon Tabasco sauce or to taste
12 ounces medium-size shrimp, peeled and deveined
1 cup diced lean ham

1. Bring the stock, bay leaf, and thyme to a boil in a 2-quart saucepan over medium-high heat. Add the rice, return to a boil, then reduce the heat to low and cook, covered, for 20 minutes without removing the lid. Remove from the heat and allow to stand for 10 more minutes before removing the lid.

2. While the rice is cooking, combine the onion, bell pepper, and garlic in a large skillet and cook, covered, over low heat until the

onion is soft and translucent, about 15 minutes. Stir occasionally and add a little water or stock, if necessary, to prevent scorching.

3. To the onion mixture, add the tomatoes, plus all of the juice from the can, the salt, pepper, and Tabasco. Mix well and bring to a simmer over medium-low heat. Add the shrimp and cook only until the shrimp become opaque and turn pink, about 2 to 3 minutes. Stir in the rice and ham, mix well, and heat to the desired serving temperature.

MAKES 4 SERVINGS

Each serving contains approximately 327 calories; 184 mg cholesterol; 4 g fat; 1270 mg sodium.

BAYOU BOUNTY SEAFOOD CASSEROLE

2 tablespoons corn-oil margarine
3 tablespoons unbleached all-purpose flour
¾ cup defatted chicken stock (see page 15)
½ cup nonfat milk
½ teaspoon salt (omit if using salted stock)
⅛ teaspoon freshly ground black pepper
2 large onions, chopped (4 cups)
2 cloves garlic, pressed or minced
1 medium green bell pepper, seeded and chopped (1 cup)
2 ribs celery, without leaves, chopped (¾ cup)
½ pound fresh mushrooms, sliced (about 4 cups)
12 ounces medium-size fresh shrimp, peeled and deveined
One 8-ounce package light cream cheese, softened
½ cup buttermilk
1 teaspoon Tabasco sauce
½ teaspoon red pepper flakes
12 ounces fresh crabmeat, picked over for cartilege and flaked
2 cups cooked brown rice
2 ounces reduced-fat sharp Cheddar cheese, grated (½ cup)

1. Melt 1 tablespoon of the margarine in a small saucepan. Add the flour and stir over medium heat for 1 minute. Do not brown. Add the stock and nonfat milk. Using a wire whisk, stir over medium heat until the mixture comes to a boil. Add the salt and black pepper and continue to cook for 1 minute more; set aside.

2. In a very large nonstick skillet, melt the remaining tablespoon of margarine. Add the onion, garlic, bell pepper, celery, and mushrooms, and cook, stirring occasionally, until soft. Add the shrimp and cook just until the shrimp turn opaque and pink. Drain off the liquid.

3. Combine all the ingredients except the Cheddar cheese in a large mixing bowl and mix well. Spread the mixture in a 9- by 13-inch glass baking dish that has been sprayed with nonstick vegetable coating. Sprinkle the cheese on top and bake at 350°F until bubbly, about 30 minutes.

MAKES 8 SERVINGS

Each serving contains approximately 322 calories; 134 mg cholesterol; 6 g fat; 617 mg sodium.

SOUTH AMERICAN RICE AND SHRIMP

½ *pound medium shrimp*
1 *tablespoon extra virgin olive oil*
1 *medium onion, finely chopped (1 ½ cups)*
2 *cloves garlic, pressed or minced*
4 *Roma tomatoes, peeled and diced (2 cups)*
½ *teaspoon salt*
½ *teaspoon freshly ground black pepper*
½ *jalapeño pepper seeded and minced, or to taste*
2 *cups cooked white rice*

1. Peel the shrimp, remove the veins, wash, drain, and set aside.

2. Warm the oil in a large skillet over medium heat. Add the onion and garlic and cook, stirring frequently, until the onion is soft and translucent, about 10 minutes. Add the tomatoes, salt, pepper, and jalapeño and cook, stirring occasionally, for 10 minutes more.

3. Add the shrimp and cook until they turn from translucent to opaque and are a bright pink, 3 to 4 minutes. Stir in the rice and heat through. Serve immediately.

MAKES ABOUT 5 CUPS, FOUR 1 ¼-CUP SERVINGS

Each serving contains approximately 265 calories; 111 mg cholesterol; 5 g fat; 431 mg sodium.

LEMON RICE AND SAUTÉED SCALLOPS

½ *cup brown rice, soaked overnight in water to cover*
1 *pound scallops*
4 *tablespoons fresh lemon juice*
3 *teaspoons olive oil*
1 *leek, white part only, finely chopped*
2 *teaspoons grated lemon zest*
1 ¼ *cups defatted chicken stock (see page 15)*
½ *teaspoon salt (omit if using salted stock)*
1 *clove garlic, pressed or minced*
¼ *cup freshly grated Parmesan cheese*

1. Drain and rinse the rice and set aside. Wash the scallops and pat dry with paper towels. Toss with 3 tablespoons of the lemon juice and set aside.

2. Place 1 ½ teaspoons of the oil in a saucepan over medium heat. Add the leek and 1 teaspoon of the lemon zest and cook, stirring, until the leek is soft. Add the rice and mix well. Add the stock and salt and bring to a boil. Reduce the heat to low and simmer, covered, until the liquid is absorbed and the rice is tender, about 25 minutes. Add the remaining tablespoon of lemon juice and mix well.

3. While the rice is cooking, heat the remaining 1 ½ teaspoons of oil in a nonstick skillet. Add the garlic and remaining teaspoon of lemon zest and cook over medium-low heat just until the garlic starts to sizzle. Add the scallops and cook just until they turn from translucent to opaque, 3 to 5 minutes.

4. To serve, arrange ½ cup of the rice on each of four plates. Top each serving with ¼ cup of the cooked scallops and 1 tablespoon of the Parmesan cheese.

MAKES 4 SERVINGS

Each serving contains approximately 267 calories; 41 mg cholesterol; 7 g fat; 727 mg sodium.

SCALLOPS, BEANS, AND VEGETABLES IN RED WINE

1 large onion, finely chopped (1 ½ cups)
1 clove garlic, pressed or minced
One 14 ½-ounce can ready-cut tomatoes
1 tablespoon sweet paprika
1 tablespoon sugar
½ teaspoon freshly ground black pepper
3 medium carrots, scraped and cut into ½-inch rounds (1 ½ cups)
3 leeks, white part only, cut into ½-inch rounds (¾ cup)
2 large fennel bulbs, diced (3 cups)
Two 16-ounce cans kidney beans, undrained
½ cup dry red wine
1 ½ pounds sea scallops
Chopped fresh parsley, for garnish (optional)

1. In a large pot over low heat, cook the onion and garlic, covered, until soft and translucent, 10 to 15 minutes. Stir occasionally and add a little water or stock, if necessary, to prevent scorching. Add

the tomatoes and their juice, the paprika, sugar, and pepper and cook, uncovered, for 5 minutes.

2. Add all remaining ingredients except the scallops and parsley and continue to cook, covered, over low heat until the vegetables can easily be pierced with a fork and the sauce has thickened.

3. Place the scallops on top of the vegetables and cook, covered, until the scallops turn from translucent to opaque, about 2 minutes.

MAKES 12 CUPS, EIGHT 1 ½-CUP SERVINGS

Each serving contains approximately 516 calories; 28 mg cholesterol; 1 g fat; 216 mg sodium.

SPICY SNAPPER AND BLACK BEANS

1 ½ *pounds red snapper fillets*
1 *lime*
½ *teaspoon freshly ground black pepper*
¼ *teaspoon salt*
1 *medium onion, finely chopped (1 ½ cups)*
2 *cloves garlic, pressed or minced*
1 *jalapeño pepper, seeded and finely chopped (1 tablespoon)*
¼ *cup chopped sun-dried tomatoes*
2 *teaspoons chili powder*
¾ *teaspoon ground cumin*
½ *teaspoon dried oregano, crushed*
One 16-ounce can black beans with liquid
¼ *cup nonfat sour cream substitute*
½ *cup finely chopped fresh chives or scallion tops*
2 *ounces reduced-fat Monterey Jack cheese, shredded (½ cup)*

1. Wash the fish and pat it dry. Place the fish in a glass baking dish and squeeze the juice from the lime over the top. Sprinkle with ¼ teaspoon of the pepper and the salt and refrigerate, tightly covered, for 1 hour.

2. Preheat the oven to 350°F. In a heavy skillet over low heat combine the onion, garlic, jalapeño, and sun-dried tomatoes. Cook, covered, until the onion is soft and translucent, 10 to 15 minutes. Stir occasionally and add a little water or stock, if necessary, to prevent scorching.

3. Add the remaining pepper, the chili powder, cumin, and oregano to the onion mixture and continue to cook, covered, for 5 more minutes. Remove from the heat and allow to cool.

4. In a blender combine the black beans plus all of the liquid from the can, the onion mixture, and sour cream and process until smooth. Spoon into a bowl, add the chopped chives, and mix well.

5. Spread 1 ½ cups of the bean mixture in the bottom of an 7- by 11-inch glass baking dish that has been sprayed with a nonstick vegetable coating. Place the fish on top of the beans. Spread the remaining bean mixture over the top of the fish and sprinkle with the shredded cheese. Bake in the preheated oven until the cheese is lightly browned and the fish turns from translucent to opaque, about 20 minutes.

6. To serve, divide the fish into six portions and spoon ½ cup of the sauce over the top of each serving.

MAKES 6 SERVINGS

Each serving contains approximately 282 calories; 42 mg cholesterol; 4 g fat; 400 mg sodium.

SESAME-CRUSTED SALMON ON PINK BEAN PUREE

If you don't like salmon or if you have a guest coming for dinner who is allergic to fish, this recipe is equally delicious made with chicken. Just substitute four boned and skinned chicken breast halves for the salmon.

FOR THE PUREE

½ pound dried pink beans, soaked overnight in water to cover
2 bay leaves
2 cloves garlic
½ cup dry vermouth
1 teaspoon lemon zest
½ teaspoon salt
¼ teaspoon freshly ground black pepper
¼ teaspoon dillweed, crushed
2 tablespoons extra virgin olive oil

FOR THE SALMON

One 1-pound salmon fillet
¼ cup fresh lemon juice
¼ cup unbleached all-purpose flour
Pinch of salt
Pinch of freshly ground black pepper
1 large egg white, lightly beaten
2 tablespoons sesame seeds
1 teaspoon dark sesame oil
4 sprigs fresh dill, for garnish

1. To make the puree, drain and rinse the beans. Place them in a pot and add water to cover by 2 inches. Add the bay leaves and bring to a boil over medium heat. Reduce the heat to low and simmer, covered, until the beans are tender, about 1 hour.

2. While the beans are cooking, preheat the oven to 400°F. Roast the garlic in the oven until soft, about 10 minutes. Peel and set aside. When the beans are tender, drain, reserving the cooking liquid, and discard the bay leaves.

3. Place the drained beans back in the cooking pot and add the roasted garlic, the vermouth, lemon zest, salt, pepper, and dill. Cover and simmer over low heat for 10 minutes. Remove from the heat and spoon the bean mixture into a food processor or blender container and puree. Add a little of the reserved cooking liquid, if necessary, to

make a thick puree. Slowly add the olive oil and blend well. Pour the pureed beans back into the pot to reheat.

4. To prepare the salmon, wash the fish and pat dry. Cut into four equal pieces. Pour the lemon juice over the fish and allow to marinate for 15 minutes. Combine the flour, salt, and pepper on one plate and place the egg white on another plate. Place the sesame seeds in a small bowl.

5. Dip both sides of each piece of salmon first in the flour, shaking off the excess, and then in the egg whites. Sprinkle each side of the fish with ¾ teaspoon of the sesame seeds, pressing them in with your fingers. Heat the sesame oil in a nonstick skillet. Carefully place the salmon in the skillet and cook over medium-high heat about 1 to 2 minutes per side; do not overcook.

6. To serve, spoon ¾ cup of the bean puree onto each of four plates and place a piece of salmon in the middle of the purée. Top each serving with a sprig of fresh dill.

MAKES 4 SERVINGS

Each serving contains approximately 581 calories; 75 mg cholesterol; 23 g fat; 955 mg sodium.

SPINACH AND SHRIMP QUESADILLAS

1 bunch (10 ounces) fresh spinach
¼ cup minced scallions
¼ cup chopped fresh tomato
¼ cup drained, rinsed, and mashed canned pinto beans
1 clove garlic, pressed or minced
1 tablespoon fresh lemon juice
½ teaspoon ground cumin
2 ounces reduced-fat Monterey Jack cheese, shredded (½ cup)
2 tablespoons low-fat ricotta cheese
2 tablespoons minced cilantro (fresh coriander)

1 cup cooked shrimp
Freshly ground black pepper, to taste
4 soft corn or whole-wheat flour tortillas
Mexican Salsa (see page 23) (optional)

1. Rinse the spinach thoroughly, remove the stems and large veins, and pat dry. Chop the spinach and combine it with the scallions, tomato, beans, garlic, lemon juice, and cumin in a medium skillet over low heat. Cook the vegetables, stirring occasionally, until all the liquid is absorbed, about 5 minutes.

2. Transfer the vegetable mixture to medium bowl and add ¼ cup of the Monterey Jack cheese, the ricotta cheese, cilantro, and shrimp. Mix well and season with pepper to taste.

3. Divide the vegetable mixture between two of the tortillas, spreading evenly over the entire surface. Sprinkle the remaining Monterey Jack cheese evenly over the mixture and place the remaining tortillas on top of the cheese to make two quesadillas.

4. Preheat the oven to 250°F. Heat a nonstick skillet over low heat and cook the first quesadilla until lightly browned on each side and the cheese is melted. Place the cooked quesadilla in the oven to keep warm while cooking the second quesadilla. Keep the quesadillas in the warm oven until time to serve. Cut each quesadilla into 8 wedges and serve warm with salsa on the side, if desired.

MAKES 4 SERVINGS, 4 WEDGES EACH

Each serving contains approximately 256 calories; 71 mg cholesterol; 5 g fat; 505 mg sodium.

CHICKEN AND POULTRY

❧

CHICKEN AND NOODLE STEW

❧

1 pound boneless, skinless chicken thighs

½ teaspoon salt

½ teaspoon freshly ground black pepper

⅛ teaspoon red pepper flakes

1 tablespoon canola oil

1 medium onion, finely chopped (1 ½ cups)

½ pound fresh mushrooms, sliced (2 cups)

2 medium carrots, scraped and cut into ½-inch rounds

1 small red bell pepper, seeded, and diced

4 Roma tomatoes, cut into 1-inch cubes

1 cup dry white wine

½ cup defatted chicken stock (see page 15)

¾ teaspoon dried tarragon, crushed
½ teaspoon dried thyme, crushed
8 ounces egg noodles
¼ cup packed chopped fresh parsley
1 cup frozen peas, thawed

1. Remove all visible fat from the chicken and cut into 1-inch cubes. Toss well with the salt, pepper, and red pepper flakes. Warm the oil in a large nonstick skillet over medium-high heat. Add the chicken and stir-fry just until the chicken is no longer pink. Remove the chicken from the skillet with a slotted spoon and set aside. Reduce the heat to low.

2. Cook the onion and mushrooms in the same skillet over low heat, covered, until the onion is soft and translucent, about 10 minutes. Add the carrots, bell pepper, tomatoes, wine, stock, tarragon, and thyme, and continue to cook, covered, until the carrot can be easily pierced with a fork, about 15 minutes.

3. Add the noodles to the vegetable mixture and cook, covered, for 10 more minutes. Add the chicken, parsley, and peas and cook until heated through, about 3 to 5 minutes.

MAKES 10 CUPS, SIX 1 ⅔-CUP SERVINGS

Each serving contains approximately 359 calories; 99 mg cholesterol; 8 g fat; 332 mg sodium.

FARFALLE WITH CHICKEN AND CAPERS

12 ounces boneless, skinless chicken breast halves
½ teaspoon salt
¼ teaspoon freshly ground black pepper
⅛ teaspoon red pepper flakes
2 tablespoons extra virgin olive oil
2 cloves garlic, pressed or minced
4 teaspoons drained capers
6 Roma tomatoes, peeled and diced (3 cups)
2 tablespoons chopped fresh oregano or 1 teaspoon dried, crushed
2 tablespoons chopped fresh Italian parsley
¼ cup defatted chicken stock (see page 15)
1 pound farfalle, cooked al dente
6 tablespoons freshly grated Romano cheese

1. Remove all visible fat from the chicken and cut into ½-inch strips. Cut each strip diagonally into ½-inch lengths and toss with the salt, pepper, and red pepper flakes. Set aside.

2. Heat the oil in a skillet over medium-high heat. Add the garlic and cook just until it sizzles. Add the chicken and stir-fry just until the chicken is no longer pink. Remove the pan from the heat and remove the chicken from the pan with a slotted spoon and set aside.

3. To the same pan, add the capers, tomatoes, oregano, and parsley. Reduce the heat to medium and return the pan to the stove. Cook, stirring frequently, for 5 minutes. Add the cooked chicken and the stock, mix well, and cook until heated through, about 5 minutes.

4. Toss the thoroughly drained cooked pasta with the chicken mixture until well combined. Sprinkle 1 tablespoon Romano cheese over the top of each serving.

MAKES ABOUT 10 CUPS, SIX 1 ⅔-CUP SERVINGS

Each serving contains approximately 362 calories; 93 mg cholesterol; 9 g fat; 369 mg sodium.

CHICKEN MANICOTTI

3 tablespoons plus 1 teaspoon corn-oil margarine
1 clove garlic, pressed or minced
½ cup unbleached all-purpose flour
2 ¼ cups defatted chicken stock (see page 15)
1 ½ cups nonfat milk
1 teaspoon dried marjoram, crushed
½ teaspoon dried oregano, crushed
½ teaspoon paprika
½ teaspoon salt (omit if using salted stock)
⅛ teaspoon freshly ground black pepper
Dash of ground cayenne pepper
4 ounces reduced-fat sharp Cheddar cheese, shredded (1 cup)
¾ cup chopped celery
¾ cup chopped onion
3 cups shredded cooked skinless chicken
12 manicotti shells, cooked according to package instructions

1. Melt 3 tablespoons of the margarine in a large saucepan over medium heat. Add the garlic and cook just until it starts to sizzle. Add the flour and stir for 1 minute, being sure not to brown the flour. Add the chicken stock and milk and, using a wire whisk, stir the mixture until it comes to a boil. Add the marjoram, oregano, paprika, salt, pepper, and cayenne and continue to cook and stir for 1 minute more.

2. Preheat the oven to 350°F. Remove all but 2 cups of the sauce and set it aside. To the remaining 2 cups of sauce, add the cheese and stir over low heat until it melts; set aside.

3. Melt the remaining margarine in a skillet over medium heat. Add the celery and onions and cook, stirring occasionally, until the onion is soft and translucent, 10 to 15 minutes. Combine with the chicken and the reserved sauce without the cheese.

4. Carefully fill each cooked manicotti shell with approximately ⅓ cup filling and place them in a 9- by 13-inch baking dish sprayed with nonstick vegetable coating. Pour the cheese sauce evenly over the manicotti and bake until hot and bubbly, 20 to 30 minutes.

MAKES SIX 2-MANICOTTI SERVINGS

Each serving contains approximately 265 calories; 49 mg cholesterol; 12 g fat; 584 mg sodium.

CHICKEN À LA RAINE

This is a recipe my daughter-in-law served at a family dinner party. She called it "Chicken a La La" because no one had been able to come up with another name. Since her name is Laraine, I renamed it for her and we continue to enjoy making it at home.

¼ cup fresh lemon juice
1 tablespoon extra virgin olive oil
½ teaspoon salt
½ teaspoon freshly ground black pepper
4 boneless, skinless chicken breast halves (1 pound)
2 ounces sun-dried tomatoes, cut in half (2 cups)
1 tablespoon olive oil
3 cloves garlic, pressed or minced
One 16-ounce can artichoke hearts, drained and halved
12 black olives, pitted and halved
¼ cup chopped fresh basil
1 teaspoon fresh rosemary leaves
4 ounces part-skim mozzarella cheese, cut into 1-inch cubes
¾ pound fettuccine, cooked al dente
1 ounce Parmesan cheese, freshly grated (¼ cup)

1. Combine the lemon juice, extra virgin olive oil, and ¼ teaspoon

each of the salt and pepper and mix well. Pour over the chicken breast halves, cover tightly, and marinate for at least 1 hour in the refrigerator. Remove the chicken from the marinade and grill or cook under a preheated broiler just until the chicken is no longer pink, 2 to 3 minutes per side.

2. Pour boiling water over the sun-dried tomatoes and allow to stand for 10 minutes. Drain thoroughly and set aside.

3. Place the olive oil in a large skillet over medium heat. Add the garlic and cook just until it sizzles. Add the remaining salt and pepper, the artichoke hearts, olives, and sun-dried tomatoes, and mix well. Cook, stirring, for 2 minutes, add the basil and rosemary, and mix well. Add the mozzarella cheese and mix well again. Immediately remove the mixture from the heat or the cheese will become tough.

4. To serve, place 1 cup of the pasta on each of four plates. Place a grilled chicken breast half on top of each mound of pasta. Top each piece of chicken with about ⅔ cup of the vegetable and cheese mixture. Sprinkle each serving with a tablespoon of the grated Parmesan cheese and serve.

MAKES 4 SERVINGS

Each serving contains approximately 570 calories; 94 mg cholesterol; 17 g fat; 760 mg sodium.

CHICKEN SPAGHETTI FROM "SCRATCH"

One 3-pound chicken
¼ cup (½ stick) corn-oil margarine
½ cup unbleached all-purpose flour
2 cups defatted chicken stock (see apge 15)
1 ½ cups nonfat milk
½ teaspoon salt (omit if using salted stock)
¼ teaspoon freshly ground black pepper
1 medium onion, chopped (1 ½ cups)
1 medium green bell pepper, seeded and chopped (1 cup)
½ cup chopped fresh mushrooms
2 ribs celery, without leaves, chopped (½ cup)
2 cloves garlic, chopped
4 ounces part-skim mozzarella cheese, grated (1 cup)
4 ounces fat-reduced Cheddar cheese, grated (1 cup)
1 pound spaghetti

1. The day before serving this dish, gently boil the chicken in plenty of water to cover until the breast juices no longer run pink and the meat springs back to the touch, about 45 minutes. Remove the chicken from the broth and place the broth in the refrigerator to allow the fat to congeal on the top. When cool enough to handle, remove the skin and bones from the chicken and chop into bite-size pieces. Refrigerate, tightly covered, to be used later in the recipe.

2. The following day melt 3 tablespoons of the margarine in a large saucepan over medium heat. Add the flour and stir for 1 minute; do not brown. Add the stock and milk and, using a wire whisk, stir until it comes to a boil. Add the salt and pepper and continue to cook for 1 minute more; set the sauce aside.

3. In a large skillet, melt the remaining margarine. Add the onion, bell pepper, mushrooms, celery, and garlic, and cook over medium heat, stirring, until the onion is tender. Combine the cheeses and set aside ½ cup for the topping. Add the remaining cheese, the sauce, and the chicken to the vegetables and mix well.

4. Preheat the oven to 350°F. Remove and discard the congealed fat from the top of the broth and boil the spaghetti in it for 8 minutes. Drain well and add to the vegetable mixture. Place in a 13- by 9-inch baking dish sprayed with nonstick vegetable coating and bake for 30 minutes. Sprinkle the reserved ½ cup of cheese over the top and return to the oven until melted.

MAKES EIGHT 1 ½-CUP SERVINGS

Each serving contains approximately 450 calories; 65 mg cholesterol; 16 g fat; 421 mg sodium.

LIGHTENED CHICKEN FETTUCCINE ALFREDO

1 tablespoon corn-oil margarine
1 tablespoon extra virgin olive oil
1 pound boneless, skinless chicken breast halves, cut into ¾-inch cubes (scant 2 cups)
3 scallions, chopped (½ cup)
¼ cup minced shallots
3 cloves garlic, minced
1 tablespoon cornstarch
1 cup low-fat (2%) milk
2 ounces Romano cheese, grated (½ cup)
12 ounces fresh mushrooms, thinly sliced (4 cups)
One 16-ounce can whole tomatoes, drained and diced
1 teaspoon onion powder
1 teaspoon salt
½ teaspoon freshly ground black pepper
2 tablespoons dried basil, crushed
1 pound fettuccine, cooked al dente
⅓ cup freshly grated Parmesan or Romano cheese

1. Heat the margarine and oil in a large skillet over medium heat. Add the chicken, scallions, shallots, and garlic and cook, stirring, until the chicken is no longer pink.

2. Stir the cornstarch into 2 tablespoons of the milk. Add to the skillet along with the remaining milk, the Romano cheese, mushrooms, tomatoes, onion powder, salt, and pepper. Bring to a boil over high heat, then reduce the heat to medium and simmer until the sauce is slightly thickened, 5 to 10 minutes, then stir in the basil and remove from the heat.

3. Toss the hot cooked pasta with the sauce and sprinkle each serving with 2 teaspoons grated Parmesan or Romano cheese.

MAKES EIGHT 1 ¼-CUP SERVINGS

Each serving contains approximately 388 calories; 43 mg cholesterol; 8 g fat; 582 mg sodium.

POULET GENEVIERE

If you are unfamiliar with flaming a recipe by igniting the alcohol, proceed with caution. Be sure you are in tight-fitting clothing to avoid accidentally igniting a loose sleeve or blouse and wear protective hot pad–type gloves. Dried juniper berries are available in most supermarkets in the gourmet section or with the other spices.

3 tablespoons corn-oil margarine
6 boneless, skinless chicken breast halves (1 ½ pounds)
½ cup gin
3 tablespoons juniper berries, crushed and put through a sieve
1 small clove garlic, pressed or minced
1 teaspoon tomato paste
¼ cup unbleached all-purpose flour
1 cup defatted chicken stock (see page 15)
¾ cup low-fat (2%) milk
10 to 12 ounces lemon-garlic pasta, cooked al dente (see note below)
2 tablespoons freshly grated Parmesan cheese

1. Preheat the oven to 350°F. Melt 1 ½ tablespoons of the margarine in a large skillet over low heat. Cook the chicken for 5 minutes, turning once. In a separate pan, heat the gin just until it starts to steam. Carefully ignite it and pour it over chicken in the skillet. When the flames subside, remove the chicken from the skillet.

2. Add the remaining margarine to the skillet along with the juniper berries and garlic. Cook 5 minutes over low heat. Using a wire whisk, stir in the tomato paste and flour to make a smooth paste. Add the chicken stock all at once and cook 5 more minutes, stirring. Slowly add the milk, stirring until completely combined.

3. Spray a 9- by 13-inch glass baking dish with nonstick vegetable coating and spread the noodles over the bottom of the dish. Lay the chicken on top and pour the sauce over the chicken. Bake until hot and bubbly, 20 to 25 minutes. Sprinkle 1 teaspoon cheese over each piece of chicken and brown under the broiler.

MAKES 6 SERVINGS

Each serving contains approximately 426 calories; 111 mg cholesterol; 10 g fat; 264 mg sodium.

Note:

If you can't find lemon-garlic pasta in the gourmet section of your market, toss 4 ½ cups cooked spaghetti or linguine with 1 teaspoon grated lemon zest and a minced or pressed clove of garlic.

SHERRIED CHICKEN STIR-FRY ON SESAME CHUKA SOBA NOODLES

Dark sesame oil and rice vinegar are available in almost any supermarket, either in the gourmet section, the ethnic foods section, or next to the other oils and vinegars. Soba noodles are also available in most supermarkets and in all oriental markets.

2 tablespoons reduced-sodium soy sauce

3 tablespoons dry sherry

2 teaspoons sugar

2 teaspoons minced peeled fresh ginger

3 cloves garlic, minced (1 tablespoon)

1 pound boneless, skinless chicken breast halves, cut into 1-inch strips

1 tablespoon rice vinegar

2 teaspoons cornstarch

2 tablespoons dark sesame oil

4 scallions, cut diagonally into 3-inch pieces

4 ounces fresh mushrooms, thinly sliced (1 cup)

¼ pound fresh asparagus, tough stems trimmed and cut into 2-inch pieces

1 medium red bell pepper, seeded and cut lengthwise into thin strips (1 cup)

One 16-ounce can pineapple chunks, in natural juice, drained

12 ounces dry soba noodles

1. In a shallow pan, combine the soy sauce, sherry, sugar, ginger, and garlic and mix well. Add the chicken strips and mix until they are well coated. Refrigerate, tightly covered, and allow to marinate for at least 30 minutes.

2. Remove the chicken from the marinade and set aside. To the marinade add the rice vinegar and cornstarch and stir until the cornstarch is completely dissolved; set aside.

3. Heat a wok or large heavy skillet until hot. Add 1 tablespoon of the oil and the chicken and stir-fry over medium-high heat for 1 minute. Add the vegetables, pineapple, and marinade mixture and stir-fry until the vegetables are crisp-tender, about 3 more minutes.

4. Cook the noodles in rapidly boiling water for 2 minutes. Drain well and toss with the remaining tablespoon of oil. To serve, place 1 cup noodles in a ring on each of four plates. Top with 2 cups of the chicken mixture.

MAKES FOUR 3-CUP SERVINGS

Each serving contains approximtely 610 calories; 66 mg cholesterol; 9 g fat; 1001 mg sodium.

POST-HOLIDAY PASTA

If you're looking for a way to use up your holiday bird this recipe is the perfect solution. I suggest serving this with wide eggless noodles, but you can certainly substitute 8 cups of any other pasta you prefer or happen to have on hand.

2 cups defatted chicken stock (see page 15)
½ teaspoon salt (omit if using salted stock)
¼ teaspoon freshly ground black pepper
¼ cup dry sherry
2 tablespoons cornstarch
One 12-ounce can evaporated skimmed milk
½ cup freshly grated Parmesan cheese
1 teaspoon fresh lemon juice
2 cups chopped cooked skinless turkey (or other leftover meat)
1 pound wide eggless noodles, cooked according to package instructions
1 tablespoon extra virgin olive oil

1. Place the stock in a saucepan over medium-high heat. Add the salt, pepper, and sherry and bring to a boil, then reduce the heat to a simmer.

2. Combine the cornstarch and canned milk and stir until the cornstarch is dissolved. Slowly add it to the simmering liquid, stirring constantly with a wire whisk. Continue to stir until slightly thickened. Remove from the heat and add the cheese, lemon juice, and chopped turkey. Mix well and cover to keep warm.

3. Toss the pasta with the oil. Place 1 cup of cooked pasta on each of eight warm plates. Top each serving with ½ cup of the sauce mixture.

MAKES EIGHT 1 ½-CUP SERVINGS

Each serving contains approximately 304 calories; 30 mg cholesterol; 5 g fat; 333 mg sodium.

FETTUCCINE AND TURKEY

3 quarts water
Salt (optional)
1 pound fettuccine
2 tablespoons plus 2 teaspoons corn-oil margarine
2 leeks, white part only, finely chopped
1 medium onion, finely chopped (1 ½ cups)
⅓ cup dry white wine
½ cup defatted chicken stock (see page 15)
½ teaspoon salt (omit if using salted stock)
⅛ teaspoon ground cayenne pepper
1 ½ cups low-fat (2%) milk, scalded
1 teaspoon fresh lemon juice
4 cups diced cooked turkey, without the skin
2 ounces Parmesan cheese, freshly grated (½ cup)

1. Put the water in a large pot, add some salt, and bring to a boil. Cook the fettuccine in the boiling water for 8 minutes. Drain, rinse with hot water, and again drain thoroughly. Stir in 2 teaspoons of the margarine and set aside.

2. Preheat the oven to 400°F. Melt the remaining margarine in a large skillet. Add the leeks, onion, wine, stock, and ½ teaspoon salt and bring to a boil. Reduce the heat to low and simmer, uncovered, until reduced by half.

3. Stir in the cayenne pepper and milk a little at a time, and continue to simmer until the sauce is smooth, slightly thickened, and reduced by one fourth.

4. Remove from the heat and add the lemon juice and turkey and mix well. Put half of the fettuccine in the bottom of a 3-quart casserole that has been sprayed with nonstick vegetable coating. Spoon half of the sauce over the top. Put the remaining fettuccine on top and spoon on the remaining sauce. Bake until hot and bubbly, 10

to 15 minutes. Sprinkle the top of each serving with 1 tablespoon Parmesan cheese.

MAKES EIGHT 1 ½-CUP SERVINGS

Each serving contains approximately 365 calories; 49 mg cholesterol; 10 g fat; 352 mg sodium.

Note:

This may be made in advance and heated just before serving. If you are doing this, bake in a preheated 350°F oven until the sauce is bubbling, 25 to 30 minutes.

TURKEY, PASTA, AND THREE-CHEESE CASSEROLE

1 pound ground turkey
1 medium onion, chopped (1 ½ cups)
1 clove garlic, pressed or minced
One 16-ounce can tomato sauce
1 teaspoon sugar
½ teaspoon salt
¼ teaspoon freshly ground black pepper
1 cup low-fat ricotta cheese
One 8-ounce package Neufchâtel cheese, softened
¼ cup light sour cream
2 scallions, chopped
1 pound ziti, cooked al dente
¼ cup freshly grated Parmesan cheese

1. Preheat the oven to 350°F. Cook the turkey, onion, and garlic in a large nonstick skillet over medium heat until lightly browned. Stir in the tomato sauce, sugar, salt, and pepper. Remove from the heat and set aside.

2. Combine the ricotta, softened Neufchâtel, sour cream, and scallions in a blender or food processor and process until well mixed.

3. Spray an 11- by 7-inch baking dish with nonstick vegetable coating. Spread half the cooked pasta in the bottom and top with half the turkey mixture. Cover with the cheese mixture, then the remaining pasta. Cover with the remaining turkey mixture, sprinkle the Parmesan cheese over the top, and bake until hot and bubbly, about 30 minutes.

MAKES 8 SERVINGS

Each serving contains approximately 462 calories; 76 mg cholesterol; 16 g fat; 756 mg sodium.

SCANDINAVIAN TURKEY MEATBALLS

2 tablespoons corn-oil margarine
1 medium onion, finely chopped (1 ½ cups)
1 cup fresh whole-wheat bread crumbs (2 slices)
¾ teaspoon salt
1 ½ teaspoons caraway seeds
1 teaspoon ground allspice
¾ teaspoon ground nutmeg
½ teaspoon freshly ground black pepper
1 ½ pounds ground turkey
1 ⅓ cups nonfat milk
2 large egg whites, lightly beaten
2 tablespoons unbleached all-purpose flour
½ cup defatted chicken stock (see page 15)
12 ounces medium eggless noodles, cooked according to package instructions

1. Melt ½ tablespoon of the margarine in a large heavy skillet over low heat. Add the onion and cook, covered, until soft and translucent, 10 to 15 minutes. Remove the cover and increase the heat

to medium. Continue to cook the onion, stirring constantly, until lightly browned.

2. Spoon the cooked onion into a large bowl. (Do not wash skillet.) Add to the onion the bread crumbs, salt, caraway seeds, ¾ teaspoon of the allspice, ½ teaspoon of the nutmeg, and ¼ teaspoon of the pepper. Mix well. Add the turkey, ⅓ cup of the milk, and the egg whites and mix thoroughly. Divide the mixture into thirty-six 1-ounce balls. Heat the skillet used for the onions and brown the meat balls on all sides over medium heat. Reduce the heat to low and cook the meatballs, covered, for 10 more minutes.

3. While the meatballs are cooking, melt the remaining margarine in another pan over medium heat. Add the flour and cook, stirring constantly, for 2 minutes; do not brown. Add the stock and the remaining allspice, nutmeg, and pepper, and mix well. Slowly add the remaining milk, stirring until slightly thickened. Remove the meatballs from the skillet with a slotted spoon and place them in the gravy. Reduce the heat to low and cook, covered, for another 10 minutes.

4. To serve, spoon 1 cup of the meatballs and gravy over 1 cup cooked noodles.

MAKES SIX 2-CUP SERVINGS

Each serving contains approximately 362 calories; 84 mg cholesterol; 13 g fat; 615 mg sodium.

SMOKED TURKEY AND GOAT CHEESE LASAGNA

½ cup chopped sun-dried tomatoes
1 large onion, finely chopped
2 cloves garlic, pressed or minced
1 pound fresh mushrooms, sliced (4 cups)
One 14-ounce can water-packed artichoke hearts, drained and quartered
3 cups low-fat ricotta cheese
4 ounces goat cheese, crumbled (1 cup)
½ cup nonfat milk
6 ounces smoked turkey, diced (1 ½ cups)
4 ounces part-skim mozzarella, grated (1 cup)
1 pound lasagna noodles, cooked al dente

1. Pour hot water over the sun-dried tomatoes and allow to stand for 10 minutes. Drain well and set aside.

2. Combine the onion, garlic, and mushrooms in a heavy pan and cook, covered, over very low heat for 20 minutes. Stir occasionally and add a little water or stock, if necessary, to prevent scorching. Uncover and continue to cook, stirring frequently, until almost all the liquid is absorbed, about 10 minutes. Remove from the heat and stir in the drained sun-dried tomatoes and the artichoke hearts. Set aside.

3. Place the ricotta and goat cheeses in a large bowl and mix well with a fork or pastry blender. Add the milk and mix well. Remove 1 cup of the mixture and set aside for the last layer. Add the turkey to the remaining cheese mixture and mix well.

4. Preheat the oven to 350°F. Spoon one third of the mushroom mixture into the bottom of a 13- by 9-inch baking dish which has been sprayed with nonstick vegetable coating. Top with a layer of the cooked noodles and then a layer of half of the cheese and turkey mixture. Repeat with another layer of each and finish with one more layer

of noodles. Cover the noodle layer with the reserved cup of the cheese mixture and sprinkle the grated mozzarella cheese evenly over the top.

5. Bake in the preheated oven until bubbly and the top is lightly browned, about 40 minutes.

MAKES 12 SERVINGS

Each serving contains approximately 335 calories; 36 mg cholesterol; 10 g fat; 319 mg sodium.

TURKEY LASAGNA ROLLS

This recipe is a variation on the classic layered lasagna. It is not only delicious, it makes both an attractive and unusual presentation.

FOR THE FILLING

1 tablespoon extra virgin olive oil
1 small Japanese eggplant, diced (1 cup)
1 medium onion, finely chopped (1 ½ cups)
2 cloves garlic, pressed or minced
½ pound ground turkey breast
1 small red bell pepper, seeded, and diced (¾ cup)
½ teaspoon dried thyme, crushed
¼ teaspoon dried oregano, crushed
¼ teaspoon salt
¼ teaspoon freshly ground black pepper
½ cup low-fat ricotta cheese

FOR THE SAUCE

½ medium onion, finely chopped (¾ cup)

1 clove garlic, pressed or minced

1 cup finely chopped fennel

½ teaspoon fennel seeds

½ teaspoon dried thyme, crushed

¼ teaspoon dried oregano, crushed

¼ teaspoon salt

¼ teaspoon freshly ground black pepper

One 14 ½-ounce can ready-cut tomatoes, undrained

6 lasagna noodles, cooked al dente

3 ounces part-skim mozzarella cheese, grated (¾ cup)

1. To make the filling, warm the olive oil in a large saucepan. Add the eggplant and stir-fry over medium-high heat until lightly browned. Remove the eggplant from the pan and set aside. To the same pan, add the onion and garlic and cook, covered, over low heat until the onion is soft and translucent, 10 to 15 minutes. Stir occasionally and add a little water or stock, if necessary, to prevent scorching. Add the turkey, red bell pepper, thyme, oregano, salt, and pepper and cook over medium heat, stirring frequently, until the turkey is done, about 10 minutes.

2. Place half of the filling mixture into a food processor and set the other half aside. Add the ricotta cheese and blend in the food processor until smooth. Combine the two filling mixtures and mix well. Put the filling mixture aside.

3. Preheat the oven to 350°F. To make the sauce, cook the onion, garlic, and fennel over low heat, covered, until the onion is soft and translucent, 10 to 15 minutes. Stir occasionally and add a little water or stock, if necessary, to prevent scorching. Add the fennel seeds, thyme, oregano, salt, pepper, and the tomatoes and their juice. Cook, uncovered, until hot and bubbly, about 15 more minutes. Spread half (1 ½ cups) of the sauce in the bottom of a 13- by 9-inch glass baking dish and set aside the remaining sauce for the topping.

4. To make the rolls, spread each cooked noodle with ⅓ cup of the filling mixture. Top with 2 tablespoons of grated cheese and carefully roll up like a jelly roll. Place each roll, seam side down, on top of the

sauce in the baking dish. Top each roll with ¼ cup of the remaining filling and cover with the remaining sauce. Cover, and bake in the preheated oven for 15 minutes. Uncover and bake until lightly browned, an additional 5 to 10 minutes.

MAKES 6 SERVINGS

Each serving contains approximately 194 calories; 42 mg cholesterol; 9 g fat; 352 mg sodium.

SWEET CHICKEN AND RICE CABBAGE ROLLS

FOR THE SAUCE

1 large head cabbage
2 medium onions, finely chopped (3 cups)
One 28-ounce can ready-cut tomatoes
½ cup defatted chicken stock (see page 15)
2 tablespoons firmly packed dark brown sugar
½ teaspoon salt
½ teaspoon freshly ground black pepper

FOR THE FILLING

½ medium onion, finely chopped (¾ cup)
1 medium carrot, scraped and finely chopped (½ cup)
1 pound ground chicken
2 tablespoons firmly packed dark brown sugar
½ teaspoon dried rosemary, crushed
½ teaspoon dried thyme, crushed
¼ teaspoon salt
¼ teaspoon freshly ground black pepper
1 ½ cups cooked brown rice
¾ cup black seedless raisins
2 large egg whites, lightly beaten

1. Remove the core from the whole cabbage. Place the cabbage cored side down in a large pan and add water to a depth of 2 inches. Bring to a boil over medium heat, reduce the heat to low and cook, covered, for 10 minutes. Remove the cabbage from the pan and carefully remove 12 whole leaves for the cabbage rolls, and set them aside. Chop the remaining cabbage to use in the sauce.

2. To make the sauce, place the onions in a heavy skillet over low heat and cook, covered, until soft and translucent, 10 to 15 minutes. Stir occasionally, and add a little water or stock, if necessary, to prevent scorching. Add the remaining sauce ingredients, including the chopped cabbage, and simmer, covered, for 45 minutes.

3. While the sauce is cooking, make the filling. Cook the onion and carrot in a skillet over low heat, covered, until the onion is soft and the carrot is tender. Stir occasionally, and add a little water or stock, if necessary, to prevent scorching. Remove from the pan to a large mixing bowl. In the same skillet over medium heat, stir-fry the chicken with the brown sugar, rosemary, thyme, salt, and pepper until the chicken is no longer pink. Add the chicken mixture to the onion mixture along with the rice, raisins, and egg whites, and mix well.

4. Preheat the oven to 350°F. Spray a 9- by 13-inch glass baking dish with nonstick vegetable coating. To make the rolls, place ⅓ cup of the filling mixture on each cabbage leaf. Fold both sides of each leaf over the filling and place seam side down in the prepared baking dish (or place 2 rolls in each of six au gratin dishes). Pour the sauce evenly over all of the rolls (or 1 cup of sauce for each au gratin dish). Cover the dish with a lid or aluminum foil and bake until hot and bubbly, 40 minutes.

MAKES 12 ROLLS, 6 SERVINGS

Each serving contains approximately 350 calories; 48 mg cholesterol; 4 g fat; 720 mg sodium.

CHICKEN CASSEROLE

2 tablespoons corn-oil margarine
1 clove garlic, pressed or minced
6 tablespoons unbleached all-purpose flour
1 ¼ cups defatted chicken stock (see page 15)
1 cup nonfat milk
½ teaspoon salt (omit if using salted stock)
⅛ teaspoon freshly ground black pepper
4 cups diced cooked chicken, without the skin
¼ cup reduced-calorie mayonnaise
4 medium ribs celery, without leaves, diced (2 cups)
2 tablespoons chopped onion
2 tablespoons fresh lemon juice
2 cups cooled cooked rice
¼ cup sliced almonds, toasted in a 350°F oven until golden brown, 8 to
   10 minutes

1. Melt the margarine in a medium-size saucepan over medium heat. Add the garlic and cook just until it starts to sizzle. Add the flour and stir for 1 to 2 minutes; do not brown. Add the stock and milk and, with a wire whisk, stir until the mixture comes to a boil. Add the salt and pepper and continue to cook for 1 minute more.

2. In a large mixing bowl, combine the sauce with the chicken, mayonnaise, celery, onion, lemon juice, and rice. Mix well and pour into a casserole sprayed with nonstick vegetable coating. Top with the toasted almonds and bake until hot and bubbly, 50 to 60 minutes.

MAKES SIX GENEROUS 1-CUP SERVINGS

Each serving contains approximately 399 calories; 83 mg cholesterol; 17 g fat; 449 mg sodium.

CHEESE-GLAZED CHICKEN AND RICE

¼ *cup unbleached all-purpose flour*
2 *teaspoons sweet paprika*
1 *teaspoon salt*
8 *boneless, skinless chicken breast halves*
2 *teaspoons corn-oil margarine*
1 *tablespoon canola oil*
½ *cup dry sherry* / PORT FRESH MUSHROOMS
2 *teaspoons cornstarch*
1 ½ *cups low-fat milk*
⅔ *cup dry white wine*
2 *tablespoons fresh lemon juice*
4 *ounces fat-reduced Swiss cheese, grated (1 cup)*
4 *cups cooked rice, at serving temperature*

1. Combine the flour, paprika, and ½ teaspoon of the salt in a bag. Coat the chicken by shaking several pieces at a time in the bag. Place the margarine and oil in a large skillet over medium heat. Add the chicken and cook until lightly browned on both sides. Add the sherry and cook, covered, until the chicken is no longer pink inside, 10 to 15 minutes. Remove the chicken from the pan and keep it warm.

2. Combine the cornstarch and milk and stir until the cornstarch is completely dissolved. Gradually stir the milk mixture and the remaining salt into the pan drippings and cook over medium heat, stirring occasionally, until slightly thickened, about 10 minutes. Add the wine and lemon juice and stir until heated through.

3. Place the chicken back into the sauce mixture and sprinkle each piece with grated cheese. Cover and cook over low heat until the cheese melts and the mixture is hot and bubbly.

4. To serve, place ½ cup hot rice on each of eight plates. Top with a piece of chicken and about ¼ cup of the sauce.

MAKES 8 SERVINGS

Each serving contains approximately 256 calories; 81 mg cholesterol; 9 g fat; 432 mg sodium.

SWEET 'N' SOUR BAKED CHICKEN

⅓ cup chopped dehydrated onion
¼ cup firmly packed dark brown sugar
½ teaspoon onion powder
½ teaspoon salt
¼ teaspoon Kitchen Bouquet
½ cup prepared tomato sauce
¼ cup red wine vinegar
One 8-ounce can crushed pineapple, in natural juice
1 teaspoon cornstarch
¼ cup water
6 boneless, skinless chicken breast halves (1 ½ pounds)
3 cups cooked brown rice, at serving temperature

1. Preheat the oven to 350°F. In a medium-size nonreactive saucepan, combine the onion, brown sugar, onion powder, salt, Kitchen Bouquet, tomato sauce, vinegar, and pineapple with its juice. Bring to a boil, then simmer over low heat, stirring constantly, for 5 minutes.

2. Dissolve the cornstarch in the water and add it to the sauce. Continue to cook and stir until the sauce is slightly thickened.

3. Spray a 9- by 13-inch glass baking dish with nonstick vegetable coating. Lay the chicken in the dish and spread the sauce on top. Bake, uncovered, for 30 minutes.

4. To serve, place ½ cup of the cooked rice on each of six warm plates. Top with a chicken breast half and spoon some of the sauce over the top.

MAKES 6 SERVINGS

Each serving contains approximately 264 calories; 97 mg cholesterol; 4 g fat; 410 mg sodium.

CHICKEN-ALMOND CASSEROLE

¼ cup chopped almonds
¾ cup fresh mushrooms, chopped
½ cup cooked brown rice
1 cup shredded skinless cooked chicken (3 ½ ounces)
1 tablespoon seeded and minced green bell pepper
⅔ cup canned evaporated skimmed milk
⅓ cup defatted chicken stock (see page 15)
1 large egg white, lightly beaten
Dash of salt
Dash of ground cayenne pepper
½ cup soft whole-wheat bread crumbs (1 slice bread)
2 teaspoons corn-oil margarine, melted

1. Preheat the oven to 350°F. Lightly spray a small casserole with nonstick vegetable coating. Place the almonds on a baking sheet and toast in the oven until golden brown, 8 to 10 minutes. Watch carefully, as they burn easily.

2. While the almonds are toasting, place the mushrooms in a microwave-safe bowl and cover with waxed paper. Microwave on high 1 minute (or steam over rapidly boiling water 2 to 3 minutes).

3. Combine all ingredients except the bread crumbs and melted margarine in the casserole dish and mix well. Mix together the bread crumbs and melted margarine and sprinkle the crumb mixture over the top. Bake until the top is golden and the casserole is hot and bubbly, about 30 minutes.

MAKES 2 SERVINGS

Each serving contains approximately: 400 calories; 48 mg cholesterol;
16 g fat; 289 mg sodium.

CHICKEN-PECAN QUICHE

1 ½ cups cooked brown rice
4 ounces reduced-fat sharp Cheddar cheese, grated (1 cup)
¼ cup very finely chopped pecans
½ teaspoon sweet paprika
¼ cup canola oil
¾ cup liquid egg substitute
One 8-ounce carton nonfat sour cream substitute
½ cup defatted chicken stock (see page 15)
2 cups chopped cooked chicken, without the skin
⅓ cup minced onion
¼ teaspoon salt
¼ teaspoon dillweed
3 to 4 drops hot pepper sauce or to taste
8 pecan halves

1. Preheat the oven to 350°F. Combine the rice, ½ cup of the cheese, the chopped pecans, and paprika, then stir in the oil. Set aside one fourth of the rice mixture and press the remainder into the bottom and up the sides of a 9-inch pie plate that has been sprayed with non-stick vegetable coating. Bake for 10 minutes; set aside to cool. Reduce the oven temperature to 325°F.

2. Combine the egg substitute, sour cream substitute, and stock. Stir in the chicken, remaining cheese, onion, salt, dill, and hot sauce. Pour into the prepared crust and sprinkle with the reserved rice mixture. Top with the pecan halves and bake until set and the top is golden, for 45 minutes.

MAKES ONE 9-INCH QUICHE, 8 SERVINGS

Each serving contains approximately 289 calories; 40 mg cholesterol; 18 g fat; 248 mg sodium.

MICROWAVE CHICKEN À LA KING

1 tablespoon corn-oil margarine
¾ cup sliced fresh mushrooms
⅓ cup seeded and chopped green bell pepper
2 tablepoons unbleached all-purpose flour
¼ teaspoon salt
1 ½ cups canned evaporated skimmed milk
2 cups diced cooked chicken, without the skin
2 tablespoons sliced pimiento
1 ½ tablespoons dry sherry
2 teaspoons fresh lemon juice
½ teaspoon sweet paprika
2 cups cooked rice, at serving temperature

1. In a microwave-safe casserole, microwave the margarine, mushrooms, and bell pepper, uncovered, at full power until soft, 2 to 4 minutes. Stir in the flour, salt, and milk. Microwave, uncovered, until thickened and bubbly, another 2 to 4 minutes.

2. Add the chicken, pimiento, sherry, lemon juice, and paprika and cook until thick and creamy, 1 ½ to 3 minutes more at full power. Serve a generous cup of the chicken mixture over ½ cup of the rice for each serving.

MAKES FOUR 1 ½-CUP SERVINGS

Each serving contains approximately 403 calories; 69 mg cholesterol; 13 g fat; 333 mg sodium.

TANDOORI CHICKEN WITH FRAGRANT BASMATI RICE

Look for whole cardamom pods and tandoori paste in Indian markets or in a specialty gourmet market. The tandoori paste will give the chicken the smoky flavor associated with the foods cooked in an Indian tandoor oven over a smoky fire.

1 cup plain nonfat yogurt
3 cloves garlic, pressed or minced
1 tablespoon fresh lemon juice
2 tablespoons tandoori paste
1 teaspoon salt
4 teaspoons finely chopped peeled fresh ginger
6 boneless, skinless chicken breast halves
1 tablespoon canola oil
1 medium onion, finely chopped (1 ½ cups)
2 cups basmati rice, washed and drained
6 black peppercorns
6 cloves
6 cardamom pods
½ teaspoon curry powder
½ teaspoon turmeric
1 ½ cups defatted chicken stock (see page 15)
Cilantro (fresh coriander) leaves for garnish (optional)

1. Combine the yogurt, garlic, lemon juice, tandoori paste, ½ teaspoon of the salt, and 2 teaspoons of the fresh ginger, and mix well. Pour over the chicken and coat each piece thoroughly. Cover and refrigerate for several hours or overnight.

2. Place the oil in a heavy pan over medium heat. Add the onion and cook, stirring occasionally, until soft and translucent, 10 to 15 minutes. Add the remaining ingredients, except the chicken, stock, and garnish, and mix well. Add the stock and bring to a boil. Reduce

the heat to low and cook, covered, for 20 minutes. Do not remove the lid! Remove from the heat but do not uncover for 10 more minutes.

3. While the rice is cooking, preheat the oven to 350°F. Remove the chicken from the marinade, place it in a baking dish that has been sprayed with nonstick vegetable coating, and bake until tender, about 15 minutes. Serve over the rice and garnish with cilantro leaves, if desired.

MAKES 6 SERVINGS

*Each serving contains approximately 440 calories; 69 mg cholesterol; 5 g fat;
841 mg sodium.*

TURKEY WITH A FUTURE

3 tablespoons corn-oil margarine
1 clove garlic, pressed or minced
2 ounces fresh mushrooms, finely chopped
6 tablespoons unbleached all-purpose flour
1 ½ cups defatted chicken stock (see page 15)
1 cup nonfat milk
½ teaspoon salt (omit if using salted stock)
⅛ teaspoon freshly ground black pepper
1 pound cooked skinless turkey, cubed (3 cups)
4 hard-cooked large egg whites, diced
4 large ribs celery, without leaves, chopped (2 cups)
½ medium onion, finely chopped (½ cup)
⅔ cup uncooked instant brown rice
2 tablespoons fresh lemon juice
2 tablespoons reduced-calorie mayonnaise
Dash of ground cayenne pepper
Four 1-ounce slices fresh whole-grain bread, finely crumbled (3 cups)

1. Melt 2 tablespoons of the margarine in a 10-inch skillet over medium heat. Add the garlic and mushrooms and cook, stirring, until the mushrooms are soft. Add the flour and stir for 1 to 2 minutes; do not brown. Add the stock and milk and stir with a whisk until the mixture comes to a boil. Add the salt and pepper, and cook 1 minute more. Set the sauce mixture aside.

2. Preheat the oven to 375°F. In a large mixing bowl, combine the turkey, chopped egg whites, celery, onion, rice, lemon juice, mayonnaise, cayenne pepper and half the bread crumbs. Add the sauce mixture and mix well.

3. Pour into a 9- by 13-inch baking dish sprayed with a nonstick vegetable coating and spread the remaining bread crumbs over the top. Melt the remaining margarine and drizzle it over the top. Bake until the top is golden and the sauce is bubbly, 30 to 35 minutes.

MAKES EIGHT 1 ½-CUP SERVINGS

Each serving contains approximately: 300 calories; 46 mg cholesterol; 10 g fat; 430 mg sodium.

WINTER WILD RICE AND TURKEY

¼ *cup wild rice*
2 *cups cold water*
½ *teaspoon salt*
1 *teaspoon fennel seeds*
1 *teaspoon canola oil*
½ *medium onion, finely chopped (¾ cup)*
1 *cup finely chopped fennel bulb*
1 *clove garlic, pressed or minced*
1 *large egg white, lightly beaten*
¼ *teaspoon freshly ground black pepper*
¼ *teaspoon dried rosemary, crushed*
¼ *teaspoon dried thyme, crushed*
⅛ *teaspoon ground nutmeg*
½ *teaspoon grated lemon zest*
1 *tablespoon finely chopped fresh parsley*
1 *tablespoon finely chopped fennel tops*
1 *large golden Delicious apple, peeled, cored, and diced*
¼ *cup unsweetened apple juice*
2 *cups warm diced cooked turkey, without the skin*

1. Combine the wild rice, water, and ¼ teaspoon of the salt in a heavy saucepan and bring to a rapid boil. Reduce the heat to low and cook, covered, for 30 minutes. Remove from the heat but leave covered until the rice is tender, another 20 to 30 minutes. Drain and set aside.

2. Place the fennel seeds in a large dry hot skillet and cook them, stirring constantly, until they are lightly browned. Add the oil and mix well. Then add the onion, fennel bulb, and garlic and cook, covered, over low heat until soft, 10 to 15 minutes. Stir occasionally, and add a little water or stock, if necessary, to prevent scorching. Set aside.

3. Preheat the oven to 325°F. In a medium-size bowl, combine the egg white, the remaining salt, the pepper, rosemary, thyme, nutmeg, lemon zest, parsley, and fennel tops and mix well. Add the apple

and cooked rice and mix well. Add the onion-fennel mixture to the bowl and again mix well. Spoon into a small casserole or a loaf pan which has been sprayed with nonstick vegetable coating. Pour the apple juice over the mixture, cover tightly with a lid or aluminum foil, and bake for 1 hour. Uncover, stir in the warm cooked turkey, and allow to stand for 15 minutes before serving.

MAKES FOUR 1 ¼-CUP SERVINGS

Each serving contains approximately 236 calories; 53 mg cholesterol; 5 g fat; 396 mg sodium.

TARRAGON CHICKEN AND WHITE BEANS

2 tablespoons corn-oil margarine
4 tablespoons unbleached all-purpose flour
¾ cup defatted chicken stock (see page 15)
½ cup nonfat milk
1 tablespoon canola oil
6 boneless, skinless chicken breast halves
8 ounces fresh mushrooms, sliced (3 cups)
1 clove garlic, pressed or minced
1 cup dry white wine
1 cup water
One 15-ounce can small white beans, drained
½ cup low-fat (2%) milk
¾ teaspoon salt
1 teaspoon dried tarragon, crushed
¼ teaspoon freshly ground black pepper
2 tablespoons chopped scallions
2 tablespoons chopped fresh parsley

1. Preheat the oven to 350°F. Melt 1 tablespoon of the margarine in a medium-size saucepan over medium heat. Add 3 tablespoons of the flour and stir for 1 minute; do not brown. Add the chicken stock and nonfat milk. Using a wire whisk, stir the mixture

over medium heat until it comes to a boil. Continue to cook 1 minute more; set aside.

2. Heat the remaining margarine in a large skillet along with the canola oil. Add the chicken and brown over medium heat, about 5 minutes on each side. Remove the chicken and place in a 4-quart glass baking dish sprayed with nonstick vegetable coating.

3. In the same skillet, cook the mushrooms and garlic over medium heat, stirring, until the mushrooms are soft, 5 minutes. Stir in the remaining tablespoon flour, the sauce from step one, the wine, water, and drained beans. Simmer over low heat, stirring, until thickened, about 10 minutes. Stir in the low-fat milk, the salt, tarragon, and pepper. Pour over the chicken and bake, uncovered, until the chicken is tender and the sauce is bubbly, for 1 hour. Sprinkle with scallions and parsley and bake 5 more minutes.

MAKES 6 SERVINGS

Each serving contains approximately 361 calories; 70 mg cholesterol; 9 g fat; 658 mg sodium.

CAPON BREAST, PINK LENTILS, AND PEARL ONIONS

1 cup (8 ounces) dried pink lentils, soaked overnight in water to cover
1 clove clove, pressed or minced
1 shallot, minced (1 tablespoon)
3 cups defatted chicken stock (see page 15)
12 pearl onions (4 ounces), peeled
Four 6- to 7-ounce skinless capon breasts
1 tablespoon dried oregano, crushed
1 tablespoon dried thyme, crushed
2 teaspoons finely chopped fresh rosemary
½ teaspoon salt

¼ teaspoon freshly ground black pepper
4 sprigs fresh thyme or rosemary
4 crusty rolls

1. Rinse and drain the lentils and set aside.

2. In a heavy pot over low heat cook the garlic and shallot, covered, until soft, about 5 minutes. Stir occasionally and add a little water, if necessary, to prevent scorching. Add the stock and lentils and simmer, covered, until the lentils are tender, about 30 minutes.

3. While the lentils are cooking, preheat the oven to 350°F. Place the onions in a 9-inch pie plate or small casserole. Lightly spray them with a nonstick vegetable coating and cover tightly with a lid or aluminum foil. Bake for 20 minutes. Uncover and bake until golden brown, 15 to 20 minutes more.

4. Season the capon breasts with the oregano, thyme, chopped rosemary, salt, and pepper and broil under a preheated broiler until the juices run clear, about 20 minutes. Do not overcook.

5. To serve, spoon ¾ cup of the cooked lentils onto each plate. Place a broiled capon breast beside the lentils and garnish with roasted onions and a sprig of fresh thyme. Serve with a crusty roll.

MAKES 4 SERVINGS

Each serving contains approximately 378 calories; 121 mg cholesterol; 7 g fat; 648 mg sodium.

MOROCCAN CHICKEN AND CHICK-PEAS

1 tablespoon canola oil

4 whole chicken thighs, skinned and all visible fat removed

1 medium onion, thinly sliced

1 teaspoon ground cumin

1 teaspoon sweet paprika

½ teaspoon salt

½ teaspoon powdered saffron, dissolved in 1 tablespoon hot water

2 cups defatted chicken stock (see page 15)

8 ounces dried garbanzo beans (chick-peas), soaked overnight in water to cover and drained

2 cups cooked brown rice, at serving temperature

¼ cup finely chopped fresh parsley

2 tablespoons fresh lemon juice

1. Place the oil in a large pot over medium heat. Add the chicken thighs and cook until a golden brown on all sides. Add the onion, cumin, paprika, and salt and cook, stirring, until the onion is soft, about 10 minutes.

2. Reduce the heat to low and add the dissolved saffron, chicken stock, and garbanzo beans. Cook, covered, stirring occasionally, until the beans are tender, about 1 ½ hours.

3. Place ½ cup of the rice on each of four plates. Top with a cooked chicken thigh and spoon the sauce and beans over the top.

MAKES 4 SERVINGS

Each serving contains approximately 474 calories; 57 mg cholesterol; 11 g fat; 616 mg sodium.

SPICY THREE BEAN AND TURKEY STEW

2 cloves garlic
1 tablespoon olive oil
1 medium onion, finely chopped (1 cup)
8 ounces ground turkey
One 15-ounce can pinto beans, drained
One 15-ounce can white beans, drained
One 15-ounce can black beans, drained
¾ cup beer
4 Roma tomatoes, diced
1 jalapeño pepper, seeded and finely chopped
1 teaspoon dark brown sugar
½ teaspoon freshly ground black pepper
½ teaspoon Liquid Smoke (see note on page 217)
6 tablespoons chopped cilantro (fresh coriander)

1. Preheat the oven to 400°F. Place the garlic in a pie plate and roast for 10 minutes. Remove from the oven and allow to cool, then peel and mash the garlic cloves with a fork.

2. Warm the oil in a large skillet over medium-low heat. Add the onion and garlic and cook, stirring frequently, until the onion is soft and translucent, 10 to 15 minutes. Add the turkey and cook, stirring frequently, until the turkey is no longer pink, about 5 minutes more.

3. Stir in all remaining ingredients, except the cilantro, and bring to a boil. Reduce the heat to low and simmer, uncovered, for 30 minutes. Remove from the oven and allow to cool slightly. To serve, spoon 1 cup of the stew into each of six bowls and sprinkle 1 tablespoon chopped cilantro over the top of each serving.

MAKES ABOUT 6 CUPS, SIX 1-CUP SERVINGS

Each serving contains approximately 372 calories; 28 mg cholesterol; 6 g fat; 676 mg sodium.

MEAT

PINOT NOIR MARINATED BEEF ON PAPPARDELLE

This recipe was developed by my friend Martha Culbertson. She and her husband, John, own the Fallbrook Winery in Fallbrook, California, and she uses their "homemade" Pinot Noir in the marinade. You can also use any dry red wine in this recipe. If you don't have a charcoal barbecue you can broil the meat in your oven.

FOR THE MARINADE

½ cup Pinot Noir
½ tablespoon whole-grain mustard
½ tablespoon chopped fresh thyme or ½ teaspoon dried, crushed

1 bay leaf
1 teaspoon salt
¼ teaspoon freshly ground black pepper
1 tablespoon extra virgin olive oil
1 ½ pounds tri tip beef

TO ASSEMBLE

1 pound pappardelle, cooked al dente (8 cups)
1 tablespoon extra virgin olive oil
¼ teaspoon freshly ground black pepper

1. Combine all the marinade ingredients and mix well. Pour the marinade over the meat, cover tightly, and refrigerate overnight.

2. The next day, remove the meat from the marinade and grill over a charcoal fire or under a preheated broiler until the desired doneness. Slice into approximately ⅛-inch-thick slices.

3. Toss the cooked pasta with the tablespoon of oil and the black pepper. To serve, place 1 cup of pasta on each of eight plates and top each serving with ½ cup sliced beef.

MAKES 8 SERVINGS

Each serving contains approximately 412 calories; 100 mg cholesterol; 22 g fat; 366 mg sodium.

BURGUNDY BEEF IN PASTA SHELLS WITH TOMATO SAUCE

FOR THE FILLING

1 tablespoon olive oil
½ medium onion, finely chopped (¾ cup)
1 small carrot, scraped and diced (½ cup)
1 pound very lean ground round beef
2 tablespoons unbleached all-purpose flour
½ teaspoon salt
¼ teaspoon freshly ground black pepper
½ teaspoon dried oregano, crushed
¼ teaspoon dried thyme, crushed
⅛ teaspoon dried rosemary, crushed
⅛ teaspoon red pepper flakes
½ cup Burgundy or other dry red wine
¼ cup freshly grated Parmesan cheese

FOR THE SAUCE

½ medium onion, finely chopped
1 clove garlic, pressed or minced
¼ teaspoon salt
¼ teaspoon freshly ground black pepper
One 14 ½-ounce can ready-cut tomatoes
16 jumbo pasta shells, cooked al dente
¼ cup freshly grated Parmesan cheese

1. To make the filling, warm the oil in a large nonstick skillet over medium heat. Add the onion and carrot and cook, stirring frequently, for 5 minutes. Add the ground meat and cook and stir for 5 more minutes. Add the flour, salt, pepper, oregano, thyme, rosemary, and red pepper flakes, and wine and mix well. Continue to cook, stirring, until the wine is absorbed. Add the cheese, mix well, remove from the heat and spoon into a mixing bowl; set aside. Do not wipe the skillet.

2. To make the sauce, in the same nonstick skillet, cook the onion and garlic, covered, over low heat until the onion is soft and translucent, about 10 minutes. Stir occasionally and add a little water or wine, if necessary, to prevent scorching. Add all remaining sauce ingredients and simmer for 10 minutes; set aside.

3. Preheat the oven to 350°F. Stuff each pasta shell with 3 tablespoons of the meat mixture. Pour half of the sauce into the bottom of an 8-inch round baking dish and place the filled shells on top of the sauce. Spoon the remaining sauce over the top, cover and bake in the preheated oven until hot and bubbly, about 25 minutes. Remove from the oven and sprinkle the Parmesan cheese over the top before serving.

MAKES 8 SERVINGS

Each serving contains approximately 374 calories; 46 mg cholesterol; 16 g fat; 364 mg sodium.

SWEET AND SOUR SHORT RIBS

½ cup unbleached all-purpose flour
2 pounds boneless short ribs, all fat removed
2 cups water
1 teaspoon salt
One 20-ounce can crushed pineapple, in natural juice
1 medium bell pepper, seeded and chopped (1 cup)
1 small onion, chopped (1 cup)
¼ cup firmly packed light or dark brown sugar
¼ cup cornstarch
2 tablespoons reduced-sodium soy sauce
⅓ cup cider vinegar
8 ounces wide eggless noodles, cooked according to package instructions

1. Put the flour and meat in a bag and shake to coat the meat. Spray a large skillet with nonstick vegetable coating and brown the

ribs over medium heat. Add the water and salt and simmer, covered, until the meat is tender, about 1 ½ hours.

2. Preheat the oven to 350°F. Drain the pineapple and measure the juice, adding enough water to make 1 cup. Set the juice aside. Add the drained pineapple, bell pepper, and onion to the meat and simmer, covered, 5 minutes. Combine the brown sugar, cornstarch, soy sauce, and vinegar with the reserved pineapple juice and mix well. Add the juice mixture to the meat and cook, stirring constantly, until thickened.

3. Combine the meat and sauce mixture with the cooked noodles in a 3-quart casserole dish. Bake until hot, about 30 minutes.

MAKES EIGHT 1 ¼-CUP SERVINGS

Each serving contains approximately 420 calories; 68 mg cholesterol; 14 g fat; 400 mg sodium.

DISH OF PLENTY

1 tablespoon corn-oil margarine
3 tablespoons unbleached all-purpose flour
¾ cup defatted chicken stock (see page 15)
½ cup nonfat milk
½ teaspoon salt (omit if using salted stock)
⅛ teaspoon freshly ground black pepper
⅛ teaspoon garlic powder
1 tablespoon dried parsley
½ pound extra-lean ground beef
1 medium onion, chopped (1 ½ cups)
3 large ribs celery, chopped
One 17-ounce can cream-style corn
½ cup cooked rice (your favorite kind)
8 ounces ring-shaped macaroni, cooked according to package instructions

1. Preheat the oven to 325°F. Melt the margarine in a saucepan over medium heat. Add the flour and stir for 1 minute; do not brown.

Add the stock and milk and, using a wire whisk, stir until it comes to a boil. Add the salt, pepper, garlic powder, and parsley. Continue to stir and cook for 1 minute more; set aside.

2. Brown the meat, onion, and celery over medium heat in a large nonstick saucepan. Drain the fat, if any. Add the corn, rice, macaroni, and stock mixture and mix well. Pour into a 1 ½- or 2-quart casserole and bake, covered, for 1 hour.

MAKES 7 CUPS, 6 SERVINGS

Each serving contains approximately 320 calories; 29 mg cholesterol; 8 g fat; 515 mg sodium.

SOUTHWESTERN BEEF AND BLACK BEAN LASAGNA

1 teaspoon cumin seeds
2 cloves garlic, pressed or minced
1 pound lean ground round beef
½ teaspoon salt
¼ teaspoon freshly ground black pepper
One 16-ounce can tomato sauce
1 teaspoon chili powder
½ teaspoon dried oregano, crushed
2 cups low-fat cottage cheese
One 4-ounce can diced green chilies
6 scallions, finely chopped (⅔ cup)
12 ounces lasagna noodles, cooked al dente
One 16-ounce can black beans, drained
8 ounces reduced-fat sharp Cheddar cheese, grated (2 cups)
1 cup nonfat sour cream substitute
Cilantro (fresh coriander) sprigs, for garnish (optional)

1. Warm a large nonstick skillet over low heat. Add the cumin

seeds and cook and stir until lightly browned and aromatic, about 2 minutes. Add the garlic, meat, salt, and pepper and cook over medium heat, stirring frequently, until the meat is brown and crumbly. Add the tomato sauce, chili powder, and oregano and simmer, uncovered, for 15 minutes. Remove from the heat and set aside.

2. Preheat the oven to 350°F. Combine the cottage cheese, chilies, and scallions and mix well. Spread one third of the meat sauce in the bottom of a 13- by 9-inch glass baking dish. Cover with a layer of noodles (about 3 rows) and top the noodles with half of the cottage cheese mixture. Spread half of the drained beans over the cottage cheese layer and sprinkle ½ cup of the Cheddar cheese over the beans.

3. Repeat the layers: sauce, noodles, cottage cheese mixture, beans, and Cheddar cheese. Cover the last layer with the remaining sauce and noodles and spread the sour cream over the top. Sprinkle with the remaining cup of Cheddar cheese and bake in the preheated oven until hot and bubbly, and lightly browned, about 40 minutes. Remove from the oven and allow to rest for about 5 minutes before cutting into 12 servings. Garnish each serving with fresh cilantro, if desired.

MAKES 12 SERVINGS

Each serving contains approximately 378 calories; 41 mg cholesterol; 13 g fat; 691 mg sodium.

MACARONI BAKE

1 pound very lean ground beef or pork
1 small onion, chopped (¾ cup)
1 clove garlic, minced or pressed
4 ounces fresh mushrooms, sliced (1 cup)
One 8-ounce can tomato sauce
One 6-ounce can tomato paste
2 tablespoons dry sherry

½ teaspoon salt

⅛ teaspoon freshly ground black pepper

One 8-ounce package elbow macaroni, cooked according to package instructions

6 ounces reduced-fat sharp Cheddar cheese, grated (1 ½ cups)

1. Preheat the oven to 350°F. Generously spray a 2-quart oven-proof casserole or baking dish with nonstick vegetable coating and set aside.

2. Lightly brown the meat in a large nonstick skillet over medium-high heat. Drain the meat very well in a colander lined with paper towels; do not wipe the skillet.

3. Reduce the heat to low and combine the onion, garlic, and mushrooms in the skillet. Cover and cook until the onion is tender, about 10 minutes. Stir occasionally and add a little water or stock, if necessary, to prevent scorching.

4. Stir the meat, tomato sauce, tomato paste, sherry, salt, and pepper into the onion mixture and simmer, covered, until the sauce is hot and bubbly, about 15 minutes. Layer half of the cooked macaroni in the bottom of the prepared baking dish. Cover with half of the meat mixture and then half of the grated cheese. Repeat with the remaining macaroni, meat, and cheese. Bake until hot and bubbly and the cheese has melted, 35 to 40 minutes.

MAKES EIGHT 1-CUP SERVINGS

Each serving contains approximately 355 calories; 53 mg cholesterol; 16 g fat; 460 mg sodium.

HARVEST MOON SUPPER

1 pound ground chicken or turkey
½ pound extra-lean ground beef
¾ cup cooked brown rice
1 large egg white, lightly beaten
1 ½ teaspoons prepared chili sauce
2 cups canned evaporated skimmed milk
One 29-ounce can water- or juice-packed yellow cling peach halves, drained
1 tablespoon firmly packed dark brown sugar
½ teaspoon ground cloves or to taste
2 tablespoons cider vinegar
1 tablespoon corn-oil margarine
⅓ cup fresh or canned mushrooms, finely chopped
3 tablespoons unbleached all-purpose flour
¾ cup defatted chicken stock (see page 15)
¼ teaspoon salt (omit if using salted stock)
Dash of garlic powder
Dash of freshly ground black pepper
1 teaspoon Worcestershire sauce

1. Preheat the oven to 350°F. Combine the meats with the rice and mix well. Combine the egg white, chili sauce, and 1 cup of the milk. Add it to the meat mixture, mix well and shape into 6 loaves. Place the loaves on a baking sheet that has been sprayed with nonstick vegetable coating and bake for 20 minutes.

2. Spray an 8-inch square baking dish with nonstick vegetable coating. Place the drained peach halves in the dish and sprinkle with the brown sugar, cloves, and vinegar. When the loaves have baked 20 minutes, place the peach mixture in the oven with the loaves and bake an additional 15 minutes.

3. While the peaches and loaves are baking, prepare the mushroom sauce. Melt the margarine in a saucepan over medium heat. Add the mushrooms and cook, stirring constantly, just until soft, 3 to 5

minutes. Add the flour and stir for 1 minute; do not brown. Add the chicken stock and ½ cup of the milk. Stir the mixture with a whisk until it comes to a boil. Add the salt, garlic powder, and pepper and cook 1 minute more. Add the Worcestershire sauce and slowly stir in the remaining ½ cup milk. Heat until steaming but do not allow the mixture to boil again.

4. To serve, place a loaf on each of six plates. Pour some sauce over each loaf and garnish with peach halves.

MAKES SIX SERVINGS

Each serving contains approximately 335 calories; 76 mg cholesterol; 11 g fat; 296 mg sodium.

STIR-FRIED RANGE BUFFALO APPETIZER WITH BLACK BEAN SAUCE AND INDIAN BREAD STICKS

The poblano chile pepper is green and about 4 inches long and can be found in the produce section of many markets. In its dried state it is called an ancho chile. The ancho chile is a deep reddish brown, and is usually available in the ethnic foods section of your market or in specialty gourmet and ethnic markets. This unusual and delicious recipe was created by Gerard Thompson, the executive chef at the famous San Yisidro Ranch in Montecito, California.

FOR THE BLACK BEAN SAUCE

¾ cup (6 ounces) black beans, soaked overnight in water to cover and drained

3 cups defatted chicken stock (see page 15)

1 ½ teaspoons chopped peeled fresh ginger

2 cloves garlic, minced or pressed

1 ancho chile, seeded and chopped

3 tablespoons sherry vinegar

½ teaspoon salt (omit if using salted stock)

FOR THE INDIAN BREAD STICKS

½ cup low-fat (2%) milk, warmed

2 teaspoons baking powder

3 scallions, finely chopped (⅓ cup)

1 teaspoon salt

1 teaspoon cracked black pepper

1 ½ cups unbleached all-purpose flour

TO COMPLETE

8 ounces buffalo or beef flank steak, trimmed of all visible fat

1 tablespoon dark sesame oil

1 tablespoon chopped peeled fresh ginger

1 clove garlic, finely chopped

1 small carrot, scraped and julienned

½ fresh poblano chile, seeded and julienned

½ small red onion, julienned

8 ounces watercress (2 bunches), stems removed, thoroughly washed, and drained (4 cups)

1. To make the sauce, combine all the sauce ingredients except the salt in a medium-size saucepan and bring to a boil over medium-high heat. Reduce the heat to low and simmer, covered, until the beans are tender, about 1 hour. Pour into a blender or food processor, add the ½ teaspoon salt, and blend until smooth.

2. While the sauce is simmering, make the bread sticks. Preheat the oven to 375°F. In a large mixing bowl, combine the milk, baking

powder, scallions, salt, and pepper. Mix well, then add the flour and knead until the dough becomes smooth, adding more flour if needed, about 3 to 5 minutes. Cover with a dishcloth and allow to rest for 30 minutes at room temperature.

3. On a lightly floured surface, divide the dough into 12 equal pieces. Shape each piece into a bread stick and place them on a baking sheet that has been sprayed with nonstick vegetable coating. Lightly spray the bread sticks with the nonstick coating and bake until golden brown on the bottom, about 10 to 15 minutes. Turn the bread sticks over and bake until the other side is lightly browned, about 5 more minutes.

4. Cut the meat against the grain into ¼-inch strips. Place the oil in a nonstick skillet or wok over high heat. Immediately add the meat and toss two times. Add the ginger and garlic and toss two more times. Add the carrot, pepper, and onion. Toss twice more and remove from the heat. Add the watercress and toss again to mix well.

5. To serve, spoon ½ cup of the sauce onto each of four warm plates. Top with 1 cup of the meat mixture and arrange 3 bread sticks in a triangular pattern on each plate.

MAKES 4 SERVINGS

Each serving contains approximately 355 calories; 53 mg cholesterol; 16 g fat; 460 mg sodium.

PORK CHILI WITH PINK BEANS

2 cups (1 pound) dried cranberry or pinto beans, soaked overnight in
water to cover and drained
4 cups defatted chicken stock (see page 15)
2 large onions, coarsely chopped (4 cups)
3 cloves garlic, finely chopped (1 tablespoon)
1 teaspoon salt (omit if using salted stock)
2 cups diced cooked pork
One 4-ounce can chopped green chilies
2 teaspoons ground cumin
1 ½ teaspoons dried oregano, crushed
1 teaspoon ground coriander
¼ teaspoon ground cloves
¼ teaspoon ground cayenne pepper
2 ounces reduced-fat Monterey Jack cheese, grated (½ cup)

1. Combine the beans, stock, half of the onions, the garlic, and
salt in a large heavy saucepan or pot and bring to a boil over medium
heat. Reduce the heat to low, cover, and simmer until the beans are
very tender, about 2 hours. If the beans start to become too dry, add
more stock, as needed. (More stock should not be needed if you are
using a heavy pan or pot.)

2. When the beans are tender, add the remaining onions, the
pork, chilies, cumin, oregano, coriander, cloves, and cayenne. Mix well
and continue to cook, covered, for 30 minutes.

3. To serve, spoon 1 ¼ cup of the chili into each serving bowl and
top with 1 tablespoon of grated cheese.

MAKES EIGHT 1 ¼-CUP SERVINGS

*Each serving contains approximately 171 calories; 17 mg cholesterol; 5 g fat;
812 mg sodium.*

PORK PROVENÇALE ON PENNE

1 medium onion, finely chopped (1 ½ cups)
3 cloves garlic, finely chopped
One 6-ounce can tomato paste
1 cup tomato juice
1 pound Roma tomatoes, peeled and diced (2 cups)
1 tablespoon sugar
1 ½ pounds very lean pork, cut into ½-inch cubes and lightly browned
    over medium-high heat
6 ounces Canadian bacon, diced
¾ cup dry red wine
½ teaspoon salt
¼ teaspoon freshly ground black pepper
Dash of ground cayenne pepper
1 pound penne, cooked al dente

1. Combine the onion and garlic in a heavy pot and cook, covered, over very low heat until soft and translucent, 10 to 15 minutes. Stir occasionally and add a little water or stock, if necessary, to prevent scorching. Add the tomato paste, tomato juice, diced tomatoes, and sugar, and mix well. Cook, covered, over very low heat, stirring occasionally, for 2 to 3 hours.

2. Add the browned pork, bacon, wine, salt, pepper, and cayenne, and mix well. Continue to cook, covered, stirring occasionally, for 2 to 3 more hours.

3. To serve, place 1 cup of the cooked pasta on each of eight warm plates and spoon ¾ cup of the meat and sauce mixture over the pasta.

MAKES EIGHT 1 ¾-CUP SERVINGS

Each serving contains approximately 476 calories; 68 mg cholesterol; 14 g fat;
630 mg sodium.

BAKED PASTA WITH TOMATOES, SHIITAKE MUSHROOMS, AND PROSCIUTTO

1 large onion, finely chopped (2 cups)

2 large cloves garlic, minced

¼ teaspoon red pepper flakes or to taste

1 teaspoon dried basil, crushed

1 teaspoon dried oregano, crushed

1 pound fresh shiitake mushrooms, stems discarded and caps sliced (8 cups)

1 tablespoon corn-oil margarine

3 tablespoons unbleached all-purpose flour

2 cups low-fat (2%) milk

Two 28-ounce cans Italian tomatoes, well drained and chopped

4 ounces thinly sliced prosciutto, cut into strips

4 ounces Fontina cheese, grated (1 cup)

4 ounces Gorgonzola cheese, crumbled (1 cup)

3 ounces Parmesan cheese, freshly grated (¾ cup)

⅔ cup minced fresh parsley

1 pound farfalle or penne

¼ teaspoon freshly ground black pepper

1. Combine the onion, garlic, red pepper, basil, oregano, and mushrooms in a large nonstick skillet over low heat. Cook, covered, until the mushrooms are tender, about 10 minutes. Stir occasionally and add a little water or stock, if necessary, to prevent scorching. Transfer the mixture to a large bowl.

2. In the same skillet, melt the margarine over medium-low heat. Whisk in the flour and cook, stirring, for 3 minutes, being careful not to brown the flour. Add the milk in a steady stream and whisk until the sauce is thickened, about 12 minutes. Pour the sauce over the mushroom mixture and add the tomatoes, prosciutto, Fontina, Gorgonzola, ½ cup of the Parmesan, and the parsley.

3. In a kettle of boiling water, cook the pasta for 5 minutes and drain well. The pasta will not be tender. Add the pasta and black pepper to the mushroom mixture and toss to combine well. Spray a 4-quart casserole with nonstick vegetable coating and transfer the pasta mixture to the casserole. Sprinkle with the remaining ¼ cup Parmesan. Bake in the middle of a 450°F oven until the top is golden, about 25 to 30 minutes.

MAKES EIGHT 1 ¾-CUP SERVINGS

Each serving contains approximately 515 calories; 48 mg cholesterol; 16 g fat; 780 mg sodium.

LASAGNA WITH BÉCHAMEL SAUCE

FOR THE MEAT SAUCE

1 cup chopped onion
½ cup chopped celery
1 clove garlic, minced
1 pound mild Italian pork sausage, removed from its casing
½ cup dry white wine
One 14 ½-ounce can chopped tomatoes (2 cups)
3 tablespoons tomato paste
2 cups defatted chicken stock (see page 15)
1 bay leaf
½ teaspoon dried oregano, crushed
½ teaspoon sugar
⅛ teaspoon ground allspice

FOR THE BÉCHAMEL SAUCE

2 tablespoons corn-oil margarine
6 tablespoons unbleached all-purpose flour
3 cups low-fat (2%) milk
Dash of ground nutmeg

TO COMPLETE

12 ounces lasagna noodles
12 ounces part-skim mozzarella cheese, grated (3 cups)
2 ounces Romano cheese, grated (½ cup)

1. To make the meat sauce, cook the onion, celery, and garlic, covered, in a large nonstick skillet over low heat until softened. Stir occasionally and add a little water or stock, if necessary, to prevent scorching. Transfer the vegetable mixture to a heavy 6-quart pot.

2. In the same large nonstick skillet, cook the sausage over medium heat until browned, stirring to break up the lumps. Pour off the fat, add the wine and boil, stirring constantly, until the wine is almost evaporated. Add the sausage to the 6-quart pot along with the remaining sauce ingredients. Simmer, uncovered, for 1 hour, stirring occasionally. Remove the bay leaf.

3. To make the béchamel sauce, while the meat sauce is simmering, melt the margarine over low heat in a heavy 3-quart saucepan. Add the flour and cook, stirring constantly, for 2 to 3 minutes, being careful not to brown the flour. Slowly pour in the milk, stirring with a wire whisk to obtain a smooth sauce. Cook until the mixture comes to a boil and thickens. Remove from the heat, stir in the nutmeg, and set aside.

4. Spray a 9- by 13-inch baking dish with nonstick vegetable coating. Preheat the oven to 350°F. Cook the lasagna in a large pot of boiling water according to the package instructions. Rinse in cold water and lay the noodles on aluminum foil or dish towels. Spread a thin layer of meat sauce on the bottom of the baking dish. Cover with one third of the noodles, then one third of the béchamel sauce, and one third of the mozzarella. Repeat two more times, ending with the mozzarella. Sprinkle the Romano cheese over the top and bake until hot and bubbly, about 30 minutes.

MAKES 10 SERVINGS

Each serving contains approximately 458 calories; 59 mg cholesterol; 22 g fat;
859 mg sodium.

ROTINI WITH ROASTED TOMATOES AND POLISH SAUSAGE

4 Roma tomatoes, quartered

4 cloves garlic, thinly sliced

1 teaspoon dried oregano, crushed

1 teaspoon dried basil, crushed

¾ teaspoon salt

¾ teaspoon freshly ground black pepper

2 tablespoons balsamic vinegar

2 tablespoons extra virgin olive oil

1 tablespoon corn-oil margarine

3 tablespoons unbleached all-purpose flour

2 ½ cups nonfat milk, at a simmer

⅛ teaspoon red pepper flakes

4 ounces Parmesan cheese, grated (1 cup)

8 ounces reduced-fat Polish sausage, cooked and diced

8 ounces rotini, cooked al dente

1. Preheat the oven to 500°F. Place the tomatoes and garlic in a shallow baking dish and sprinkle with the oregano, basil, ½ teaspoon salt and ½ teaspoon pepper. Combine the vinegar and oil and pour over the top. Place in the preheated oven until the tomatoes are caramelized, but not burned, about 8 minutes. Set aside to cool.

2. Reduce the oven temperature to 350°F. Melt the margarine in a heavy saucepan over low heat. Add the flour and cook, stirring, for 2 minutes; do not brown.

3. Remove the pan from the heat and add the simmering milk, stirring constantly with a wire whisk. Add the remaining ¼ teaspoon salt and pepper, and red pepper flakes. Return the pan to the heat and simmer, slowly, until thickened, 15 to 20 minutes, stirring occasionally. Remove from the heat and add the cheese. Mix well and set the sauce aside.

4. Spray a 2-quart casserole with a nonstick vegetable coating. Add the cooked sausage, cooked pasta, and the cheese sauce and mix well. Gently fold in the roasted tomatoes and place in the 350°F oven until bubbly, about 15 minutes.

MAKES ABOUT 6 CUPS, SIX 1-CUP SERVINGS

Each serving contains approximately 441 calories; 71 mg cholesterol; 24 g fat; 1061 mg sodium.

OLD-FASHIONED MEAT LOAF

One 8-ounce can tomato sauce
1 ½ tablespoons cider vinegar
1 ½ tablespoons brown mustard
2 ½ tablespoons firmly packed dark brown sugar
1 cup water
1 ½ pounds very lean ground round
1 cup cooked brown rice
1 medium onion, finely chopped (1 cup)
1 clove garlic, pressed or minced
1 large egg, lightly beaten
½ teaspoon salt
¼ teaspoon freshly ground black pepper
⅛ teaspoon red pepper flakes

1. Preheat the oven to 350°F. Combine ½ cup of the tomato sauce with the vinegar, mustard, and brown sugar and mix well. Add the water and again mix well. Set aside to baste the meat loaf with.

2. Combine the meat, rice, onion, garlic, egg, salt, pepper, and red pepper flakes and mix well. Add the remaining tomato sauce and again mix well. Form into a loaf and place in an 11- by 7-inch baking dish. Bake for 1 ½ hours, basting frequently with the sauce mixture.

MAKES 12 SERVINGS

Each serving contains approximately 191 calories; 60 mg cholesterol; 12 g fat; 282 mg sodium.

TERIYAKI STEAK AND RICE

🦐

¼ cup reduced-sodium soy sauce

1 tablespoon cider or red wine vinegar

2 small cloves garlic, chopped

One ½-inch piece fresh ginger, peeled and chopped

One 6-ounce can frozen unsweetened apple juice concentrate, thawed

2 scallions, finely chopped

2 pounds flank steak, all visible fat removed

4 cups cooked long-grain white or brown rice, at serving temperature

4 cups snow peas, ends notched and steamed until crisp-tender, about 3 minutes

1. Combine the soy sauce, vinegar, garlic, ginger, and apple juice concentrate in a blender and process until smooth. Stir in the scallions. Makes about 1 cup marinade.

2. Place the steak in a glass baking dish and pour the marinade over the steak. Marinate 10 to 24 hours in the refrigerator, turning occasionally to distribute the marinade evenly over the meat.

3. Cook the meat over hot charcoal or under a preheated broiler, 4 to 5 minutes on each side for medium-rare. Slice thinly across the grain before serving with ½ cup rice and ½ cup snow peas.

MAKES 8 SERVINGS

Each serving contains approximately 365 calories; 59 mg cholesterol; 12 g fat; 332 mg sodium.

SWEET AND SOUR PORK

One 8-ounce can pineapple chunks, in natural juice
2 teaspoons cornstarch
¼ teaspoon salt
3 tablespoons cider vinegar
2 tablespoons sugar
1 ½ teaspoons reduced-sodium soy sauce
2 cups cubed cooked pork, all visible fat removed
1 small onion, thinly sliced (1 cup)
1 small green bell pepper, seeded and thinly sliced (¾ cup)
2 ounces fresh mushrooms, sliced (½ cup)
One 6-ounce can water chestnuts, drained, rinsed, and thinly sliced
2 cups cooked brown rice, at serving temperature

1. Drain the juice from the pineapple chunks and pour it into a large saucepan. Set the pineapple chunks aside to add later. Add the cornstarch to the juice and stir until it is thoroughly dissolved. Add the salt, vinegar, and sugar and cook over medium heat, stirring constantly, until the sauce has thickened.

2. Remove from the heat and add the reserved pineapple, soy sauce, and pork. Mix well and allow to stand for 1 hour. Add the onion, bell pepper, mushrooms, and water chestnuts and cook over medium heat until the vegetables are just crisp-tender, about 3 minutes.

3. To serve, place ½ cup rice on each of four warm plates and spoon 1 cup of the pork mixture over the top.

MAKES FOUR 1 ½-CUP SERVINGS

Each serving contains approximately 321 calories; 39 mg cholesterol; 5 g fat; 256 mg sodium.

PORK SATÉ ON SEASONED RICE

Dark sesame oil and peanut butter provide this dish with its exotic flavor. Look for the oil in the ethnic section of your market, or the gourmet section, or in any oriental market. Unhomogenized or old-fashioned peanut butter is available right next to the regular peanut butter, as well as in health food stores and the health food section of many markets.

> *2 tablespoons unhomogenized (old-fashioned) peanut butter*
> *2 tablespoons fresh lemon juice*
> *3 tablespoons reduced-sodium soy sauce*
> *1 tablespoon firmly packed dark brown sugar*
> *¼ teaspoon red pepper flakes*
> *1 clove garlic, pressed or minced*
> *½ cup finely chopped onion*
> *1 pound boneless pork loin, all visible fat removed and cut into ½-inch cubes*
> *2 cups cooked brown rice*
> *¼ cup finely chopped cilantro (fresh coriander)*
> *¼ cup finely chopped fresh chives or scallion tops*
> *1 tablespoon dark sesame oil*

1. Combine the peanut butter, lemon juice, and 1 tablespoon of the soy sauce and mix until smooth. Add the sugar, pepper flakes, garlic, and chopped onion and mix well. Add the cubed pork, mix well and allow to marinate, refrigerated, for at least 30 minutes.

2. Thread the pork onto skewers and grill over hot coals or under a preheated broiler about 8 minutes, turning frequently. (If using bamboo skewers, soak them in water for at least 1 hour to prevent burning.)

3. Combine the rice, cilantro, chives, and remaining soy sauce and mix well. Place the oil in a large heavy skillet or wok over medium-high heat and stir-fry the rice mixture until hot, 2 to 3 minutes.

4. To serve, place ½ cup of the rice mixture on each of four warm plates. Divide the skewered grilled pork on top of the rice.

MAKES 4 SERVINGS

Each serving contains approximately 391 calories; 71 mg cholesterol; 16 g fat; 451 mg sodium.

BEST BAKED BEANS

This is absolutely my favorite baked bean recipe. The secret of the fabulous flavor is the Southern "Seasoning" and the long baking time.

3 cups dried small white beans, soaked overnight in water to cover
3 tablespoons molasses
⅓ cup firmly packed dark brown sugar
2 teaspoons dry mustard
1 teaspoon salt
¼ teaspoon freshly ground black pepper
6 cups Southern "Seasoning" (see page 18)

1. Rinse, drain, and pick over the beans. Put them in a large pot and add water to cover by 2 inches. Bring to a boil, reduce the heat and simmer, covered, until the beans are tender, 60 to 90 minutes. Drain well.

2. Preheat the oven to 325°F. Combine the drained beans with all remaining ingredients and mix well. Spray a bean pot or a 2-quart casserole with a nonstick vegetable coating and spoon the bean mixture into the pot. Cover and bake for 4 hours, stirring every hour. Uncover and bake for 30 more minutes.

MAKES 8 CUPS, EIGHT 1-CUP SERVINGS

Each serving contains approximately 184 calories; negligible cholesterol; 1 g fat; 792 mg sodium.

RED BEANS AND BROWN RICE

⚹

1 pound dried red beans, soaked overnight in water to cover

2 large onions, finely chopped (3 cups)

3 cloves garlic, pressed or minced

6 scallions, finely chopped

1 medium green bell pepper, seeded, and diced

1 cup packed chopped fresh parsley

2 Roma tomatoes, peeled and diced

1 teaspoon salt

1 teaspoon freshly ground black pepper

¼ teaspoon ground cayenne pepper or to taste

1 teaspoon dried oregano, crushed

½ teaspoon dried thyme, crushed

2 bay leaves, crumbled

¼ cup cider vinegar

1 ½ tablespoons Worcestershire sauce

4 cups Southern "Seasoning" (see page 18)

3 cups cooked brown rice

1. Drain and rinse the beans. Place them in a heavy pot and add water to cover by 2 inches. Bring to a boil over medium-high heat then reduce the heat to low and cook, covered, for 1 hour.

2. While the beans are cooking, combine the onion, garlic, scallions, and bell pepper and cook, covered, over low heat until soft, 10 to 15 minutes. Stir occasionally and add a little water or stock, if necessary, to prevent scorching. Add all remaining ingredients except the Southern "Seasoning" and rice and mix well. Set aside.

3. After 1 hour remove the beans from the heat and drain well. Place them back in the pot, add the Southern Seasoning and the onion mixture and mix well. Bring to a boil over medium heat, then reduce

the heat to low and simmer, covered, for 1 more hour. Stir in the rice and cook, uncovered, for 30 more minutes.

MAKES 12 CUPS, TWELVE 1-CUP SERVINGS

Each serving contains approximately 233 calories; 4 mg cholesterol; 1 g fat; 360 mg sodium.

PORTUGUESE RED BEANS

1 large onion, finely chopped (1 ½ cups)
3 cloves garlic, pressed or minced
1 jalapeño pepper, seeded and chopped
6 ounces Canadian bacon, diced
One 14 ½-ounce can ready-cut tomatoes, drained
¼ teaspoon freshly ground black pepper
¼ teaspoon ground cinnamon
½ teaspoon chili powder
1 teaspoon ground cumin
Two 16-ounce cans red kidney beans, drained

1. Combine the onion, garlic, and jalapeño in a large pan and cook over low heat, covered, until the onion is soft and translucent, about 10 to 15 minutes. Stir occasionally and add a little water or stock, if necessary, to prevent scorching.

2. Uncover and add the Canadian bacon. Cook, stirring, for 3 minutes. Add the tomatoes, pepper, cinnamon, chili powder, and cumin. Mix well and continue to simmer for 10 minutes. Add the beans and simmer until hot and bubbly, about 10 more minutes.

MAKES ABOUT 6 CUPS, FOUR 1 ½-CUP SERVINGS

Each serving contains approximately 334 calories; 25 mg cholesterol; 5 g fat; 1446 mg sodium.

GREEN BEAN CASSEROLE

Even though we usually think of green beans as simply a vegetable, they are also legumes and, therefore, belong in this book.

Two 9-ounce packages frozen French-cut green beans, thawed and drained
1 medium onion, sliced and separated into rings (2 cups)
2 ounces Canadian bacon, cut into 1-inch pieces
¼ cup slivered blanched almonds
¼ cup sugar
¼ cup distilled vinegar
2 tablespoons canola oil
½ teaspoon salt
¼ teaspoon Liquid Smoke (see note below)

1. In a 1 ½-quart casserole, layer the beans, onion rings, Canadian bacon, and almonds.

2. In a small bowl, combine the sugar, vinegar, oil, salt, and Liquid Smoke. Mix with a wire whisk until the sugar and salt are dissolved. Pour over the layers in the casserole, refrigerate, and allow to marinate several hours or overnight.

3. Bake in a preheated 350°F oven for 45 minutes. Remove from the oven and stir before serving.

MAKES EIGHT ¾-CUP SERVINGS

Each serving contains approximately 129 calories; 4 mg cholesterol; 7 g fat; 251 mg sodium.

Note:

Liquid Smoke is usually found with the sauces, often near the barbecue sauces, since it is used to impart a "cooked over an open fire" flavor. It is simply distilled smoke essence and is all natural and perfectly safe.

BAKED BEANS

2 ounces Canadian bacon, cut into ½-inch pieces

½ pound extra-lean ground beef

1 large onion, chopped (2 cups)

½ cup prepared tomato sauce

½ cup firmly packed dark brown sugar

¼ cup white sugar

1 tablespoon Worcestershire sauce

1 tablespoon molasses

2 teaspoons cider vinegar

1 teaspoon onion powder

1 teaspoon freshly ground black pepper

½ teaspoon chili powder

⅛ teaspoon salt

One 15-ounce can butter (lima) beans, very well drained

One 15-ounce can red kidney beans, very well drained

Two 16-ounce cans small white or Great Northern beans, very well drained

1. Preheat the oven to 350°F. Cook the bacon in a large skillet over medium heat until slightly brown. Add the ground beef and onion and cook, stirring, until the beef is brown and the onion is translucent. Drain off any fat in the pan and pour the mixture into a 3- or 4-quart baking dish that has been sprayed with nonstick vegetable coating.

2. Stir all the remaining ingredients into the baking dish and bake until hot and bubbly, about 1 hour.

MAKES EIGHT 1-CUP SERVINGS

Each serving contains approximately 300 calories; 20 mg cholesterol; 4 g fat; 515 mg sodium.

BEEF AND BEAN FRITTATA

2 cups liquid egg substitute
8 ounces very lean ground beef
One 8-ounce can red kidney or pinto beans, rinsed and well drained
8 ounces reduced-fat Monterey Jack cheese, grated (2 cups)
8 ounces fresh mushrooms, sliced (2 cups)
1 cup finely chopped onion
½ cup seeded and finely chopped red bell pepper
One 4-ounce can diced green chilies
½ teaspoon freshly ground black pepper
⅛ teaspoon ground cayenne pepper or to taste
1 cup canned evaporated skimmed milk

1. Lightly grease a 9- by 13-inch glass baking dish. Pour the egg substitute into the baking dish and set aside.

2. Brown the meat in a nonstick skillet over medium heat. Drain well and spread evenly over the egg substitute. Spread the beans over the meat and top with half of the grated cheese.

3. Layer the mushrooms, onion, bell pepper, and chilies over the cheese and sprinkle with the black and cayenne peppers. Pour the milk evenly over all and top with the remaining cheese. Cover tightly and refrigerate for several hours or overnight.

4. Bake in a preheated 350°F oven until the top is lightly browned and the egg substitute is firm, about 40 to 50 minutes. Remove from the oven and let rest 5 minutes before serving.

MAKES 8 SERVINGS

Each serving contains approximately 284 calories; 23 mg cholesterol; 14 g fat; 362 mg sodium.

BRAISED LAMB SHANKS WITH GARBANZO BEANS

1 tablespoon olive oil

Four 10- to 12-ounce lamb shanks, trimmed of all visible fat and sinews

1 teaspoon salt (½ teaspoon, if using salted stock)

1 teaspoon freshly ground black pepper

1 medium onion, finely chopped (1 ½ cups)

2 cloves garlic, minced or pressed

One 28-ounce can tomato puree

4 cups defatted chicken stock (see page 15)

1 tablespoon dried oregano, crushed

1 teaspoon dried thyme, crushed

¼ teaspoon red pepper flakes

1 pound dried garbanzo beans (chick-peas), soaked overnight in water to
   cover and drained

4 medium carrots, scraped and diced

1. Preheat the oven to 325°F. Heat the olive oil in a large oven-proof pot or Dutch oven. Sprinkle the lamb shanks with ½ teaspoon of the salt and ½ teaspoon of the pepper and brown the shanks on all sides over medium-high heat.

2. Add the onion and garlic and cook, covered, over low heat until the onion is soft, 10 to 15 minutes. Stir occasionally and add a little stock, if necessary, to prevent scorching. Uncover, add the remaining ingredients except the carrots, and bring to a boil.

3. Cover and place the mixture in the oven until the meat is about to fall from the bones, about 3 ½ hours, turning the shanks every 30 minutes. Add the carrots for the last 30 minutes of cooking time.

4. To serve, carefully remove the lamb shanks from the braising liquid and place each shank in a large serving bowl. Top with the braising liquid, beans, and carrots.

MAKES 4 SERVINGS

*Each serving contains approximately 1116 calories; 190 mg cholesterol;
46 g fat; 1321 mg sodium.*

LAMB FRICASSEE WITH FIELD VEGETABLES AND GARBANZO BEANS

½ teaspoon ground cardamom

½ teaspoon ground cinnamon

½ teaspoon salt

½ teaspoon freshly ground black pepper

1 bay leaf

1 tablespoon extra virgin olive oil

2 tablespoons fresh lemon juice

1 pound lean lamb (meat from the leg is ideal), trimmed of all visible fat and cut into 1-inch cubes

1 medium onion, chopped (1 ½ cups)

3 cloves garlic, pressed or minced

8 ounces garbanzo beans (chick-peas), soaked overnight in water to cover and drained

2 cups defatted beef stock (see page 17)

½ cup diced carrot

½ cup diced celery

½ cup cauliflower florets

½ cup peeled and diced eggplant

½ cup diced cabbage

½ cup diced zucchini

1 tablespoon cornstarch

1 tablespoon water

1 cup diced fresh tomatoes

Lemon Couscous (see page 68; optional)

1. Combine the cardamom, cinnamon, salt, pepper, bay leaf, oil, and lemon juice. Mix well and pour over the lamb in a glass container. Toss thoroughly, cover, and allow to marinate in the refrigerator for several hours or overnight. Stir occasionally to distribute the marinade evenly. Serve with Lemon Couscous.

2. Combine the onions and garlic in heavy pot or soup kettle over low heat and cook, covered, until the onion is soft and translu-

cent, 10 to 15 minutes. Stir occasionally and add a little water or stock, if neccesary, to prevent scorching. Add the marinated lamb and cook, stirring, over medium-high heat until the meat is no longer pink. Add the beans along with the beef stock. Bring to a boil, reduce the heat to low, and simmer, covered, until the beans are tender, about 30 to 40 minutes.

3. Add all of the vegetables except the tomatoes and cook for 10 minutes. Dissolve the cornstarch in the water and add it to the pot along with the tomatoes and cook, uncovered, for 5 more minutes. Serve in bowls with Lemon Couscous, if desired.

MAKES SIX 1-CUP SERVINGS

Each serving contains approximately 296 calories; 48 mg cholesterol; 8 g fat; 430 mg sodium.

BREADS, ETC.

✻

BASIC PASTA

✻

This recipe yields about 1 ¼ pounds of fresh pasta. If you are not
going to make the pasta immediately, or if you have some of the
dough left over, wrap and freeze it for later use. Or, roll it out, cut it
into uniform shapes, dry it out, and then store it in an airtight container to use as you would any dried pasta. In the lemon and chive
pasta variation, instead of lemon and chives, you can substitute ½ to
1 cup, loosely packed, of your favorite fresh herb, or a combination.
Strongly flavored herbs, such as oregano or rosemary, should be used
in smaller quantities, rounding out the cup of herbs with parsley.

1 ½ cups semolina or unbleached all-purpose flour
½ teaspoon salt
1 large egg
2 large egg whites

1. In a large bowl, combine the flour and salt, stirring to blend. In a small bowl, combine the egg and egg whites and mix well. Make a well in the center of the flour and pour in the egg mixture. With a pastry blender, a fork, or your fingertips, gradually incorporate all of the flour, kneading the dough by hand until it becomes a firm ball that is shiny, smooth, and elastic. (If using a processor, follow the directions provided by your machine's manufacturer.)

2. Cover the dough with plastic wrap and allow to rest at room temperature for 20 minutes or overnight before rolling and cutting.

3. Divide into 4 equal pieces, about 5 ounces each. With the palm of your hand, flatten each piece, on a lightly floured board, into a square about 1 inch thick. With a heavy rolling pin, roll out each square to a thickness of about ⅛ inch or less, carefully lifting the dough and sprinkling a little more flour on the board to prevent sticking. Cut the dough into the desired shape. (If you prefer to use a pasta machine, follow the directions for your machine.)

4. For fettuccine, roll the dough into a jelly-roll shape. Cut into ¼-inch wide slices and quickly unroll the slices into strips to prevent them from sticking together. Wire coat hangers work well for hanging the fettuccine to dry before cooking it.

5. To cook the pasta, bring 8 quarts of water to a boil. Add the pasta and boil for 2 to 3 minutes or until the pasta is al dente, meaning it has a slight resilience when eaten. When cooked, pour the pasta into a colander and drain well. Serve immediately.

MAKES ABOUT FOUR 1-CUP SERVINGS

Each serving contains approximately 246 calories; 53 mg cholesterol; 2 g fat; 337 mg sodium.

Variations

Whole-wheat Pasta: Substitute whole-wheat flour for the semolina or unbleached flour.

Lemon and Chive Pasta: Add ½ cup loosely packed minced chives, 1 tablespoon grated lemon rind, and ½ teaspoon fresh lemon juice to the egg and egg whites. Mix well, and proceed with the recipe for basic pasta.

Eggless Pasta: Substitute 1 ½ tablespoons canola, corn, or olive oil and ¾ cup warm water for the egg and egg whites. Combine the flour, salt, and oil and blend well. Gradually add the water, kneading the dough by hand until it becomes a firm ball that is shiny, smooth and elastic. Cover and allow to rest for at least 20 minutes, then proceed with the recipe for basic pasta.

COUSCOUS CAKES

½ cup couscous
2 tablespoons unbleached all-purpose flour
¼ teaspoon baking soda
¼ teaspoon salt
½ teaspoon sugar
¾ cup buttermilk
1 large egg white, lightly beaten
1 tablespoon canola oil

1. In a medium-size bowl combine the couscous, flour, soda, salt, and sugar and mix well. In another bowl, beat together the buttermilk, egg white, and oil until well blended. Pour the liquid into the dry ingredients and mix well. The batter should be the consistency of heavy cream. If it starts to get too thick, thin with a little more buttermilk.

2. Lightly oil a large skillet or griddle and wipe almost dry with a paper towel. Warm the skillet over medium heat until a drop of water

dances on the surface before evaporating. For each cake, spoon 2 tablespoons batter into the skillet and cook until bubbles that form on the surface start to break and the bottom is a golden brown. Turn the cakes over and cook until the other side is brown, about 1 minute more.

MAKES ABOUT 12 CAKES

Each cake contains approximately 37 calories; 1 mg cholesterol; 1 g fat; 87 mg sodium.

HERBED WILD RICE AND WALNUT BREAD

¼ *cup chopped walnuts*
One ¼-ounce package active dry yeast (check date on package before using)
1 teaspoon sugar
1 ¾ cups lukewarm water
4 ½ cups unbleached all-purpose flour
1 teaspoon salt
2 tablespoons extra virgin olive oil
½ cup cooked wild rice
1 teaspoon dried thyme, crushed
½ teaspoon dried rosemary, crushed
¼ cup black seedless raisins

1. Preheat the oven to 350°F. Place the walnuts in a pie pan and toast in the preheated oven until golden brown, 8 to 10 minutes. Watch carefully, as they burn easily. Set aside. Increase the oven temperature to 400°F.

2. Combine the yeast, sugar, and warm water and mix well. Allow to stand until bubbly, about 10 minutes. Stir in the flour, salt, and oil and mix well.

3. Turn the dough onto a lightly floured board and knead until smooth and elastic, adding a little more flour, if necessary. Transfer the dough to an oiled bowl, turning to oil the entire surface. Cover and allow to rise in a warm place until doubled in bulk, 40 to 50 minutes.

4. Punch the dough down and knead in the rice, thyme, rosemary, raisins, and walnuts. Place the dough in a 13- by 9-inch baking pan that has been sprayed with nonstick vegetable coating. Spread the dough evenly within the pan, cover, and allow to rise for 30 minutes. Make "dimples" in the surface of the dough with your fingers and bake in the lower half of the preheated oven until a golden brown, about 35 minutes. Remove from the oven and allow to rest about 10 minutes before cutting into squares.

MAKES 12 SERVINGS

Each serving contains approximately 226 calories; no cholesterol; 4 g fat; 198 mg sodium.

SAVORY WILD RICE MUFFINS

These savory muffins are the perfect accompaniment to soups and salads. I like to make them in miniature muffin tins and serve them right on the plate with the soup bowl or on the side of the salad plate. This recipe makes 24 miniature or 12 standard muffins, and they freeze beautifully. If you don't have any wild rice on hand, cooked brown rice substitutes well in this recipe.

1 medium onion, finely chopped (1 ½ cups)
1 clove garlic, pressed or minced
2 cups whole-wheat flour
1 tablespoon baking powder
½ teaspoon salt
½ teaspoon freshly ground black pepper
⅛ teaspoon ground cayenne pepper
1 ½ teaspoons dried marjoram, crushed
1 large egg plus 2 large egg whites, lightly beaten
1 cup nonfat milk
¼ cup extra virgin olive oil
1 cup cooked wild rice

1. Preheat the oven to 350°F. Combine the onion and garlic in a heavy saucepan and cook, covered, over low heat until soft, 10 to 15 minutes. Stir occasionally and add a little water or stock, if necessary, to prevent scorching. Remove from the heat and set aside.

2. Combine the flour, baking powder, salt, peppers, and marjoram and mix well.

3. Combine the egg and egg whites with the milk and olive oil and mix well. Add the rice and again mix well. Pour the liquid ingredients over the dry ingredients and mix until well moistened. Do not overmix. The batter will be stiff.

4. Spray 12 standard muffin tins with nonstick vegetable coating and fill each tin with ⅓ cup batter. Bake in the preheated oven until a golden brown, 25 to 30 minutes. Allow to cool for 5 minutes before turning the muffins out to cool on a rack.

MAKES 12 MUFFINS

Each muffin contains approximately 150 calories; 18 mg cholesterol; 5 g fat; 292 mg sodium.

CURRIED CHICKEN AND RICE CAKES

These cakes are as versatile as they are delicious. You can serve them as a substitute for rolls with a soup or salad or as a light entrée. I like to serve them with chutney. For a light vegetarian entrée, substitute tempeh for the chicken. Tempeh is available in all health food stores.

½ cup whole-wheat flour
½ teaspoon baking powder
2 cups cooked brown rice
1 cup ground or finely chopped cooked chicken
½ cup finely chopped celery
⅓ cup finely chopped onion
1 tablespoon finely chopped fresh parsley

1 tablespoon reduced-sodium soy sauce
1 tablespoon fresh lemon juice
¾ cup plain nonfat yogurt
1 ½ teaspoons curry powder
3 large egg whites

1. Preheat the oven to 375°F. In a large bowl, combine the flour and baking powder and mix well. Add all the other ingredients except the egg whites and mix well.

2. Beat the egg whites until stiff but not dry and fold into the chicken and rice mixture.

3. Spray 12 standard muffin cups with nonstick vegetable coating and spoon ½ cup of the mixture into each cup. Bake until golden brown, about 35 minutes. Serve hot.

MAKES 12 CAKES

Each cake contains approximately 77 calories; 7 mg cholesterol; 1 g fat; 110 mg sodium.

ALMOND, RICE, AND RAISIN CAKE

¼ cup chopped almonds
¾ cup long-grain white rice
2 ¼ cups cold water
½ teaspoon salt
One 12-ounce can evaporated skimmed milk
½ cup firmly packed brown sugar
½ teaspoon ground cinnamon
2 tablespoons corn-oil margarine
3 large egg whites
1 large egg yolk, lightly beaten
¼ cup black seedless raisins

1. Preheat the oven to 350°F. Spray the inside of a 10-inch round cake pan with nonstick vegetable coating. Cut a round piece of parchment or waxed paper to line the bottom of the pan. Spray the paper with the nonstick vegetable coating and set the pan aside.

2. Place the almonds in a pie pan and toast them in the preheated oven until golden brown, 8 to 10 minutes. Watch carefully, as they burn easily. Set aside.

3. Combine the rice, 1 ½ cups of the cold water, and the salt in a saucepan. Bring to a boil over medium heat, reduce the heat to low, and simmer, covered, for 5 minutes. Remove from the heat and drain thoroughly.

4. Warm the milk and remaining ¾ cup water in a 2-quart saucepan over medium heat. When steam starts to show above the liquid, add the sugar, cinnamon, margarine, and drained rice and mix well. Bring to a boil, then reduce the heat to low and simmer, stirring frequently, until all the liquid is absorbed, about 20 minutes. Remove from the heat and set aside.

5. Beat the egg whites in a large bowl until firm but not stiff. Fold in the beaten egg yolk, add the toasted almonds, the raisins, and the rice mixture, folding until well blended. Spoon the mixture into the prepared cake pan and spread evenly. Bake in the preheated oven for 30 minutes.

6. Remove from the oven and cool on a rack for 20 minutes before inverting onto a plate and removing the paper. Allow to cool completely and then wrap tightly and refrigerate until cold before cutting into 16 pie-shaped wedges.

MAKES 16 SERVINGS

Each serving contains approximately 95 calories; 14 mg cholesterol; 3 g fat; 123 mg sodium.

PEANUT BUTTER BREAD

1 ¾ cups whole-wheat flour
1 teaspoon baking powder
1 teaspoon baking soda
¼ teaspoon salt
½ teaspoon ground cinnamon
½ cup unhomogenized (old-fashioned) peanut butter
½ cup honey
2 tablespoons peanut oil
1 large egg plus 2 large egg whites, lightly beaten
¼ cup nonfat milk
2 small ripe bananas, mashed (1 cup)
1 small golden Delicious apple, peeled, cored, and grated (½ cup)

1. Preheat the oven to 300°F. In a large mixing bowl combine the flour, baking powder, baking soda, salt, and cinnamon and mix well.

2. In another, smaller bowl, combine the peanut butter, honey, oil, eggs, and milk and mix well. Spoon the wet ingredients into the dry ingredients and mix just until thoroughly moistened. Do not over-mix.

3. Spoon the batter into a 9- by 5-inch loaf pan which has been sprayed with nonstick vegetable coating and bake in the preheated oven until a knife inserted in the center comes out clean, about 1 hour and 15 minutes. Remove from the oven and place on a wire rack to cool.

MAKES 16 SLICES

Each slice contains approximately 156 calories; 13 mg cholesterol; 6 g fat; 125 mg sodium.

QUICK & EASY BLACK BEAN CAKES

One 16-ounce can black beans, undrained
2 tablespoons sherry
½ teaspoon minced peeled fresh ginger
1 clove garlic, pressed or minced
4 large egg whites, lightly beaten
⅓ cup whole-wheat flour
3 scallions, finely chopped (⅓ cup)
¼ teaspoon freshly ground black pepper
1 tablespoon dark sesame oil

1. Combine the undrained beans, the sherry, ginger, and garlic in a blender and blend until smooth. Pour the bean mixture into a bowl and stir in all remaining ingredients.

2. To cook, lightly oil a griddle or frying pan and wipe off with a paper towel. Warm the pan over medium heat, until a drop of water dances on the surface before evaporating. For each bean cake spoon 2 tablespoons of batter onto the griddle and cook until lightly browned, for about 1 minute. Flip over and cook until lightly browned, about 30 seconds more. Keep the cakes warm in a covered dish until all cakes are made.

MAKES ABOUT 16 CAKES

*Each cake contains approximately 62 calories; no cholesterol; 1g fat;
81 mg sodium.*

PEANUT BUTTER OATMEAL MUFFINS

1 ½ cups whole-wheat flour
¾ cup quick-cooking oatmeal
1 tablespoon baking powder
½ teaspoon salt
¾ cup unhomogenized (old-fashioned) crunchy peanut butter
1 tablespoon dark sesame oil
¼ cup granulated sugar
¼ cup firmly packed dark brown sugar
2 large egg whites, lightly beaten
1 cup nonfat milk
2 teaspoons pure vanilla extract

1. Preheat the oven to 375°F. Spray 12 standard muffin tins with nonstick vegetable coating and set aside. In a large mixing bowl, combine the flour, oatmeal, baking powder, and salt, mixing well.

2. In another bowl, combine the peanut butter, oil, and sugars, and mix until completely blended. Add the egg whites and mix well. Add the milk, a little at a time, blending well after each addition. Add the vanilla and again mix well.

3. Pour the liquid into the dry ingredients and mix just until the dry ingredients are moistened. Do not overmix. Immediately spoon the batter into the muffin tins and bake until a golden brown, about 20 minutes. Remove from the oven and place the tins on a rack to cool. Do not remove the muffins from the tins for 5 to 10 minutes.

MAKES 12 MUFFINS

Each muffin contains approximately 220 calories; no cholesterol; 10 g fat;
290 mg sodium.

BLACK BEAN PANCAKES FOR NACHOS

One 16-ounce can black beans
2 tablespoons minced onion
1 clove garlic, quartered
⅛ teaspoon freshly ground black pepper
⅛ teaspoon red pepper flakes
⅛ teaspoon ground cumin
2 large egg whites
½ cup unbleached all-purpose flour
1 tablespoon canola oil
½ cup nonfat milk
4 ounces reduced-fat Monterey Jack cheese, shredded (1 cup)
Mexican Salsa (see page 23; optional)

1. Place the canned beans and their liquid in a blender and puree. Add all remaining ingredients except the cheese (and salsa) and again puree. Refrigerate for 2 hours.

2. Preheat the oven to 350°F. To make the pancakes, spray a nonstick skillet with nonstick vegetable coating and warm over medium heat until a drop of water dances on the surface before evaporating. For each pancake, spoon 2 tablespoonsful of the batter into the pan and cook until bubbles form and break on the surface. Turn the pancakes over and lightly brown on the other side. If the batter becomes too thick, thin with more milk.

3. When all of the pancakes have been cooked, spread them out on a baking sheet that has been sprayed with a nonstick vegetable coating and place the baking sheet in the preheated oven. Bake until they are crisp, about 10 minutes. Remove from the oven and turn over to crisp the other side. Remove from the oven and top each pancake with 1 tablespoon of the grated cheese. Return to the oven and bake until the cheese is melted. Garnish with salsa, if desired.

MAKES 2 CUPS BATTER, 16 PANCAKES

Each pancake contains approximately 87 calories; 0 mg cholesterol; 3 g fat;
102 mg sodium.

SOUTHWESTERN CORN BREAD PIZZA

This recipe is a wonderful example of using the flavors of one cuisine with the technique of another.

FOR THE CRUST

1 cup yellow cornmeal
1 cup unbleached all-purpose flour
1 tablespoon baking powder
¼ teaspoon salt
¼ teaspoon freshly ground black pepper
½ teaspoon ground cumin
½ teaspoon chili powder
2 large egg whites, lightly beaten
1 cup nonfat milk
3 tablespoons canola oil

FOR THE TOPPING

1 medium onion, chopped (1 ½ cups)
2 cloves garlic, chopped
1 jalapeño pepper, seeded and chopped
¼ teaspoon freshly ground black pepper
½ teaspoon dried oregano, crushed
One 15-ounce can black beans
½ cup fresh or frozen corn kernels
½ cup seeded and diced bell pepper
½ cup diced tomato
6 black olives, chopped (optional)
4 ounces reduced-fat sharp Cheddar cheese, grated (1 cup)

1. To make the crust, combine all the dry ingredients in a large mixing bowl and mix well. In another, smaller bowl, combine the liquid ingredients and mix well. Pour the liquid into the dry ingredients and mix just until well moistened. Do not overmix.

2. Pour the batter into a 13-inch pizza pan which has been sprayed with a nonstick vegetable coating. Tilt the pan to spread the batter evenly over the surface.

3. Preheat the oven to 400°F. To make the sauce, place 1 cup of the chopped onion in a heavy pan. Set the remaining onion aside. Add the garlic and jalapeño and cook, covered, over low heat, until the onion is soft, about 10 to 15 minutes. Stir occasionally and add a little water or stock, if necessary, to prevent scorching. Stir in the pepper and oregano and cook, covered, for 3 more minutes.

4. Drain the beans, reserving the liquid from the can. Place the beans in a blender, add the onion mixture and puree, adding about ⅓ cup of the bean liquid, or enough to make a smooth sauce. Spread the bean sauce carefully over the top of the corn bread batter in the pizza pan.

5. Sprinkle the remaining onion, the corn kernels, bell pepper, tomato, and olives over the top of the sauce. Sprinkle the grated cheese over the top and bake in the preheated oven until the cheese is bubbly and starting to brown, about 20 minutes. To serve, cut into wedges.

MAKES 8 SERVINGS

Each serving contains approximately 328 calories; 8 mg cholesterol; 9 g fat; 422 mg sodium.

INDEX